Russ Hope was born in London in 1983 and studied at the University of Warwick. His work as a theatre director includes *Brooklyn* (Cock Tavern Theatre), *The Last Five Years* (Apollo Theatre, Shaftesbury Avenue), *Wired* and *Finishing the Hat* (King's Head Theatre), *Knickerbocker Glories* (Union Theatre, Southwark), *Lucky Nurse and other short musical plays* and *The Fix* (Edinburgh Festival) and *Square-Eyed* (Etcetera Theatre Club).

His work has been described variously as 'a revelatory experience' (*Stage*), 'a refined joy' (*TheLondonist.com*) and 'almost worth the schlep to Kilburn' (*Guardian*).

This is his first book.

Getting Directions

A Fly-on-the-Wall Guide for Emerging Theatre Directors

Russ Hope

Foreword by Dominic Cooke

NICK HERN BOOKS

London

www.nickhernbooks.co.uk

A Nick Hern Book

Getting Directions
first published in Great Britain in 2012
by Nick Hern Books Limited, The Glasshouse,
49a Goldhawk Road, London W12 8QP

Copyright © 2012 Russ Hope
Foreword copyright © 2012 Dominic Cooke

Russ Hope has asserted his moral right
to be identified as the author of this work

Designed and typeset by Nick Hern Books
Printed and bound in Great Britain
by Ashford Colour Press, Gosport, Hampshire

A CIP catalogue record for this book is available
from the British Library

ISBN 978 1 84842 182 0

MIX
Paper from
responsible sources
FSC
www.fsc.org   FSC® C011748

'You know a conjuror gets no credit when once he has explained his trick, and if I show you too much of my method of working, you will come to the conclusion that I am a very ordinary individual after all.'

Sir Arthur Conan Doyle (A Study in Scarlet)

'I hold that the opposite is true.'

Russ Hope

Contents ➡

Foreword ➡

Dominic Cooke

Of all theatre arts, directing is the most mysterious. Rehearsal rooms are, by necessity, private places. Privacy is essential to allow directors and actors to take risks, free from the self-consciousness that creeps in when an audience is present. What takes place between actor and director in the rehearsal process is informed as much by the particulars of their relationship as it is by the text and experience they bring to their work. Much of the process is unconscious and therefore hard to explain to a third party. Some of the success of a production is down to alchemy – the magic that can happen when a group of individuals gather around a particular play at a particular time. This is one of the reasons why directing practice is so hard to communicate.

Books have been written by directors about their craft. Some of these are articulate and persuasive. Recently, Katie Mitchell and Mike Alfreds have anatomised their practices in two fascinating books, and I have heard young directors referring to these as influences on their own working methods.

However, no matter how structured a director's process may seem, when it comes to the meeting between actor and director in the rehearsal room, the skilful director will adapt their approach to meet the particular needs of the actor and scene they are working on. Pragmatism is an essential tool for any director and the way that a process is applied is as significant as the process itself. The personality, passion and obsessions of each director play a crucial role in bringing a text to life. Therefore, there are as many directing processes as there are directors, and each director's experience of a particular production is unique. This is one of the reasons that theatre flourishes – there is no 'correct' way of doing it. Directing is an art not a science.

This book reveals some of the diverse approaches to directing being used by young directors today. Russ Hope gives us unprecedented access to the rehearsal rooms and thinking of some of our most interesting young directors. Each director has a unique approach to their work, a particular set of values and a singular challenge in the play and space they are animating. *Getting Directions* documents this with a judicious mix of cold objectivity, sympathy and wit. The result is an incisive kaleidoscope of rehearsal-room practice which is a useful tool for directors to borrow from and a fascinating insight for the curious. I hope it interests and informs you as much as it did me.

Acknowledgements ➡

I am indebted first and foremost to every director, artistic director, actor, stage manager, company manager, designer, marketer, usher and intern who let me into their rehearsal rooms and into the unfinished thoughts in their heads; their untidy first versions and ground plans not yet beautiful successes or heroic failures.

I am especially grateful for the freedom each director gave me to write and to prod as I saw fit. I remain amazed that they could be so engaged and interested in something peripheral to the sizeable task of making a theatre production.

Thanks also to Mark Shenton for the pep talk; to Andy Dickson at the *Guardian* for posting me a padded envelope stuffed with studies and raw interview tapes; to Rob Icke, Caroline Steinbeis and Steven Atkinson, whose interviews added to the general swirl; Louis Theroux, whose interview persona (the buffoonish Machiavelli) I stole wholesale; to my editor Matt for his guidance and his patience; to my partner Louise for guidance and patience of a different kind; and finally to the actor who hugged me, high on endorphins, having survived her first preview performance. 'Thank you for all you did,' she said, and I looked down at the bottle of complimentary beer in my hand then at my laptop, which lay sapping the theatre's Wi-Fi as it beamed the day's notes into cyberspace, and felt acutely aware that, whilst the company proved itself each day in rehearsals and now onstage, I had yet to show my hand.

'I'm not sure I did anything,' I said.

'Yes you did,' she said. 'You were here.'

Introduction ➡️
On a Lighting Gantry

It is 2005 and I am crouching in a lighting gantry, hoping I cannot be heard, hoping to remain unnoticed. I am in the studio theatre at the university I attend where, twenty feet below, the director Peter Brook is rehearsing with the actor Bruce Myers ahead of a workshop performance of a new piece.

I was looking for my phone, which I had misplaced during rehearsals for a student play, and as I walked across the lighting gantry, I realised that something was going on below. The piece is *The Grand Inquisitor*, from the chapter in Dostoyevsky's *The Brothers Karamazov* in which Jesus finds himself in the Spanish Inquisition. Myers, as the high priest, interrogates an empty chair. 'If you are God, turn these stones into bread.' I realise that, if I can stay quiet enough, I might stow away with them to Seville.

What I didn't know is that Peter Brook rehearses in French. It doesn't matter that the actor and the director are English, nor that the performance will be in English. I don't speak French. Not a word.

Brook says something to Myers. He speaks, unbroken and calm, for maybe five seconds, and Myers nods and speaks the line again: 'If you are God, turn these stones into bread.' Before, it was a threat. Now, there is compassion within, and almost a longing for God to return. The actor appears to hold two contradictory ideas in his mind at once, and the poetry of that struggle reaches all the way up to the lighting gantry.

To this day, I do not know what Brook said that could have had such a transformative effect.

This book reinvestigates that moment, broadcasting the feed from the security camera in that often sacred place, the rehearsal room.

Each chapter documents the creative process for a production by a theatremaker at the forefront of a generation of British theatre. The account is part rehearsal diary, part essay and contains the most candid interviews you will read on the challenges of working as a professional theatremaker. Each account follows a production from its inception through pre-rehearsal meetings, rehearsals, the tech process and preview performances to press night. The productions are: a new version of a Greek play, two different approaches to Shakespeare plays, a Great American Play, an adaptation of a British novel, a pantomime, a plotless live performance by a devising company and an opera. At the end, there is a short section that offers a collection of principles to help the emerging director find focus, decide which projects to pursue, and create work that excites them.

Getting Directions is a book about creative relationships, approaching problems, and learning good judgement. It is a book about a day job as much as a vocation, and craft as much as art. It aims to help you ask better questions (of yourself, of texts, of companies) and develop your own theories and process. What it does not promise is quick fixes, for all silver bullets turn out to be quicksilver. This is to say nothing of the crime that it would be to rob you of the bittersweetness of making your own mistakes, those frustrating, exhilarating steps on the path towards developing your own voice, with its own attendant quirks and tactics.

I can't drive. When people ask why, I tell them I took lessons (which is true) and was doing well (which is not true). Then, one day I convinced myself that, living in London, I would have no need of a car and, in any case, wouldn't be able to afford one (true, not true, true). Since then, I maintain, I have had no desire to drive – buses and trains are just fine, thanks (definitely not true).

The truth is: driving scared me. A car weighs a ton and can move at eighty miles an hour, yet we've decided to let almost anyone drive one. For all I know, someone might drive his car into something fragile and valuable like someone else. Or me. Unable to compartmentalise that fear, London's roads – even the quiet back roads near my parents' house – transformed into Spaghetti Junctions and mountains. The fact that I had paid attention in my lessons and knew the Highway Code meant nothing. I would have been crazy to ask my teacher to put me up for the exam, and he would have been crazy to consider it.

Driving, like any activity, requires a balance of knowledge, skill and behaviour: in this case that means knowledge of the Highway Code, the dexterity to point the car where you want it to go, and a temperament that's neither hesitant nor gung-ho. Anything less than three out of three and you'll be sitting at the bus stop, bursting with knowledge but utterly ineffective.

You could be reading this book for any number of reasons. Perhaps you have strong instincts but want to revisit first principles. Perhaps you excel in the abstract theory of directing but find yourself clamming up every time you're forced to communicate your ideas. Perhaps you want to know how to get a leg up in a saturated industry. Or perhaps you are simply beginning to think about plays as more than simply 'staged literature', and what the screenwriter Charlie Kaufmann once called 'the staggering possibilities of light, vibration and time'.

A Few Ground Rules ➡️

1. The chapters snip and pinch time. As most rehearsal processes share a common ancestor, I have focused on the elements of each process that seemed most remarkable or instructive. For example, one chapter might emphasise casting, or the tech period, whilst another passes quickly over those sections or omits them entirely. This is not to say that a conversation in one chapter did not happen in some version in another, or that each director did not have something to say about each part of the process.

2. When we are searching for answers, it can be tempting to focus on craft to the extent that we create a depersonalised system. The reality is that any work that is of value will be personal and idiosyncratic to its maker.

3. Part of the director's job is to tailor process to purpose. With that in mind, this book does not claim to give the definitive account of a director's mind or imply an unchanging process. It merely captures a particular process that worked for a particular production at a particular point in time.

4. Any comparisons I draw between individuals or processes are mine alone.

5. The gendered pronoun for a director will reflect the gender of the director in that chapter.

6. Because our focus is on directors, the protagonist of each chapter is more fleshed-out than the company. To refer to a director by name, then to 'an actor', 'the actors' or 'the company' could be interpreted as suggesting two sides of a conflict or a lone-wolf auteur against a crowd, but nothing could be further from the truth. I cannot overstate the contribution of actors, as individuals and as a group, to each production.

Matthew Dunster

Troilus and Cressida
by William Shakespeare
Shakespeare's Globe

Matthew Dunster directs, writes, teaches and acts – and probably in that order. He has directed new work (*Mogadishu*, Royal Exchange, Manchester; *Love the Sinner*, National Theatre; *The Frontline*, Shakespeare's Globe), large-scale Elizabethan productions (*Macbeth*, Royal Exchange; *Doctor Faustus*, Shakespeare's Globe) and worked on adaptations that push notions of theatricality (*Saturday Night Sunday Morning* and *1984*, Royal Exchange; *The Farenheit Twins*, Barbican). As a writer, his plays include *Children's Children* (Almeida Theatre) and *You Can See the Hills* (Young Vic). He teaches drama to many different groups of people, and is an associate artist of the Young Vic.

'Directing isn't about playing loads of games… it's about detail, and detail is about craft. It's taken me a long time to get to a place where I'm comfortable in my process, and where the cast are respectful but we can have fun. Getting there takes guile, graft and the help and guidance of others.'

Matthew Dunster

Paul Stocker (Troilus), Matthew Kelly (Pandarus) and
Laura Pyper (Cressida)

Troilus and Cressida by William Shakespeare

Opened at Shakespeare's Globe, London, on 22 July 2009.

Creative
Director **Matthew Dunster**
Designer **Anna Fleischle**
Composer **Olly Fox**
Choreographer **Aline David**

Cast
Ulysses **Jamie Ballard**
Paris **Ben Bishop**
Andromache **Olivia Chaney**
Hector **Christopher Colquhoun**
Agamemnon **Matthew Flynn**
Achilles **Trystan Gravelle**
Menelaus/Alexander **Richard Hansell**
Thersites **Paul Hunter**
Aeneas **Fraser James**
Pandarus **Matthew Kelly**
Priam/Calchas **Séamus O'Neill**
Cressida **Laura Pyper**
Helen/Cassandra **Ania Sowinski**
Nestor **John Stahl**
Troilus **Paul Stocker**
Diomedes/Helenus **Jay Taylor**
Patroclus **Beru Tessema**
Ajax **Chinna Wodu**

Musicians **Joe Townsend, Jon Banks, Ian East, Phil Hopkins** and **Genevieve Wilkins**

To: the cast of *Troilus and Cressida*
Date: 23 May 2009
Subject: Welcome
▶ 1 Attachment [Troilus_rehearsal_draft.doc]

Hello Cast,

I just wanted to send a note with the rehearsal script (see attached).

I have worked with some of you before, and I think the work I have done editing the script will feel pretty tame to you guys.

To those new to the way I work – don't worry about any ideas contained in the stage directions: they are first ideas and not prescriptive. Your ideas will always be better than mine and I look forward to hearing them.

My rules on approaching anything are simple: CLARITY – STORY – DRAMATIC EFFECTIVENESS. I want it to be clear and exciting.

In getting the play down from its massive 28,500 words to around 21,000, sometimes the iambic has been ruptured. Ruptured, but never disregarded. I know how it works and have only made sacrifices where I felt it would improve the chances of a modern audience understanding the text. Where I have chopped things around, the original is always there for us to go back to. Likewise, let's keep looking for cuts and places where our modern understanding of dramatic language can help us tell his brilliant story. Let's collaborate with Shakespeare. He was a populist – he would want people to get it and be excited by it.

Having spent so long getting inside the play, I am convinced of its brilliance. I can't wait to take you all inside its dark heart. Every character wriggles with complexity.

Rehearsals are simple. From day two we'll do circuit training and stretches for the first 45 mins (you'll all be dicking around in togas and sandals so it's in your best interest!) and for most of the first two weeks we will read and read and read.

Everything points to a strong Homeric show full of anachronistic surprises. I can't wait.

I'm off to Croatia in about five hours so I for one will be tanned and beautiful when we meet!

Looking forward to it.

Matthew

Shakespeare's Globe ➡️

It is an uncharacteristically warm morning on the South Bank of the Thames. An ice-cream van is parked outside the entrance to Shakespeare's Globe, its queue snaking towards the Millennium Bridge. In front of the theatre gates, a tourist photographs her son as he gives his best 'Alas, poor Yorick', a Flake '99 standing in for the skull. As the ice cream melts down his wrist, the kid accelerates his half-remembered speech: something about 'I knew him well…'

I am at the corner of New Globe Walk and Bankside, looking at Shakespeare's Globe, an oddity of wood and thatch sandwiched between the chrome and glass of twenty-first-century restaurants and bars. A blue plaque on the wall in front of me reminds passers-by that this institution, so quintessentially English, was the vision of an American, Sam Wanamaker, who founded the Globe Theatre Trust in 1970 and pursued the project until his death in 1993, four years before the theatre presented its first season.

In 2008, Dominic Dromgoole became the second artistic director of the Globe following Mark Rylance, an actor known for his shape-shifting, mercurial performances. Like Rylance, Dromgoole combines a classical appreciation of Shakespeare's work with a love of the raucous; the bearpit on which the new Globe is modelled.

Earlier in his career, Droomgoole served as artistic director of the Bush in West London, a prolific new-writing theatre, where he premiered work by writers including David Harrower and Conor McPherson.

As part of his first season, Droomgoole commissioned a piece from the playwright Ché Walker. *The Frontline* was a head-on, high-speed collision of the Globe's legacy with the present. Set in modern-day Camden, a company of hoodies, asylum seekers and lap dancers took to the Elizabethan stage with sneakers and boom boxes to celebrate and dissect all that London is and could be.

To direct *The Frontline*, Dromgoole hired Matthew Dunster.

Matthew Dunster ➡

I first meet Matthew at the Young Vic, after a matinee performance of his play *You Can See the Hills*, which he also directs. It is midweek and the theatre is two-thirds full. Matthew sits on the back row, his arms spread across the empty seats either side. As the house lights go down, he kicks his feet up on the seat in front. He reacts as if he doesn't know how the story ends, laughing at the jokes and leaning in to the tension.

After *The Frontline*, Dominic Dromgoole invited Matthew to return to the Globe, this time to direct a play by Shakespeare. Dominic suggested *Troilus and Cressida*, one of the few in the canon that the theatre had yet to produce in a full-scale production, and which Matthew hadn't read, either when Dominic suggested it or when he agreed to the job. He tells me this and he registers my surprise:

People tend not to believe me when I say that, but I wanted to do a Shakespeare play I didn't even have a sense of. I've acted in some of the others or I've read them, but I don't know anything about *Troilus and Cressida* so I can treat it as a new play, and that's exciting. Of course, once I read it, I realised how difficult it's going to be. I had to read the script twice before I understood a word of it.

I leave thinking this is bluster; the boasts of a director who wants the first notes I make to be that I have just met a 'maverick'. At home, I pull my *Complete Works* from the shelf and flick past nine hundred pages to *Troilus and Cressida*.

Damn.

I have to read it twice too before I understand much of what's going on.

A Quick History Lesson ➡

The story of *Troilus and Cressida* is ancient, and has passed through many tellers. It begins seven years into the siege of Troy, when the war has reached a stalemate. The demigods of Greek mythology – Agamemnon, Ajax, Achilles, Hector, Menelaus, Paris and Helen – are siloed in their camps, breaking the monotony with skirmishes. A Trojan prince, Troilus, falls in love with a young woman, Cressida, whose father defected to the Greeks, but their love is short-lived: the Trojan generals agree to trade Cressida for one of their own, a soldier languishing in a Greek prisoner-of-war camp.

Shakespeare probably knew the story through the versions by Chaucer and Homer. But where Chaucer treats his subjects with wry humour and sympathy, Shakespeare hunts them for vanity; where Homer sees heroes,

Shakespeare sees a boil to be lanced. In Shakespeare's version, the war is a chaos fought over a 'whore and cuckold' from which no one will learn a damned thing. Thersites, the knowing fool, says it best: 'Nothing [but lechery] holds fashion.'

Shakespeare's *Troilus and Cressida* has long confounded critics, audiences and theatremakers alike. Without a protagonist, veering between comedy and tragedy, and with an ending that raises more questions than it answers, it was consigned to that drawer marked 'problem play' where it gathered dust for best part of three hundred years. There is some suggestion that it may not even have been performed during Shakespeare's lifetime. In the late sixteenth century, the dramatist John Dryden tried to make sense of the play, only he didn't 'make sense' of it so much as edit out the bits he didn't understand, reordering scenes, adding and removing dialogue and killing Cressida in the play's final third to allow Troilus to rise as a traditional revenge hero. Dryden's *Troilus and Cressida* remained the favoured text until the play went out of fashion, remaining unperformed until the horrors of the First World War prompted society at large to reinvestigate the gulf between the ancient warriors they'd read about in books, and the unprecedented horror they now read about in the newspapers, or witnessed first-hand.

It could also be argued that modern audiences, schooled in the fractured narratives of contemporary cinema and the slow-burning ensemble stories of television, are simply better primed to respond to the play's structure. Either way, Matthew isn't interested in critical baggage. 'People obsess over whether it's a tragedy or a history play or a comedy,' he says. 'The answer seems obvious: it's all of them. If we celebrate those complications, I think the audience will accept them.'

The Text and the Space ➔

The Globe has an imposing character of its own. Half the audience stands, and performances happen in the open air without amplified sound. In the daytime, actor and audience share the sunlight – every face is visible – and the quality this creates is difficult to pin down, even to those who have worked in it. A magnetic field hums between the play and the space that Matthew would be 'a fool', he says, to ignore. A production at the Globe requires a bespoke response.

Conceiving a production, a director has two main sources of inspiration:

- The Text
- The Performance Space

Directing a production for the Globe can be a disarming experience as it robs the director of two of the main tools of contemporary theatre: recorded sound and focused light. The reason for this is an artistic policy that the theatre calls 'original practice'. Enforced to varying degrees depending on the production, original practice ensures that the audience's experience of the production reflects the aesthetics of Elizabethan theatre. Yes, the auditorium is fitted with a sprinkler system (after all, the original Globe burned down!), and yes, there may be video monitors backstage, but these are usually hidden from the audience.

Then there is the space, which is infamously exposing, large and open on three sides. Complicated sets tend to obscure many in the audience's view, and are cumbersome to set up and strike from the stage. The Globe's immune system seems to reject them as a body might reject a transplanted organ.

In an interview with the *Guardian* in 2009, Dominic Dromgoole explained how the 'well-fashioned miniature' doesn't work at the Globe: 'You have to tell big stories here… big lungs, big action, big thought.' Whilst Matthew favours stillness generally – 'I don't think an actor should move unless the character needs to' – his experience directing *The Frontline* taught him that a production at the Globe needs to keep moving, lest it exclude some section of the audience.

Does this mean that a production at the Globe must be more theatrical? Matthew grimaces at the question. He asks me if I just used 'theatrical' as a synonym for 'big'. I nod, and I think I may have stepped into a bear trap. 'West End musicals tend to be larger than performances in studios,' he says. 'Would you say that either is necessarily more *theatrical*?' 'No,' I say. 'Of course I wouldn't.' The trap closes around my ankle. 'A theatrical experience doesn't mean a diversion from something naturalistic or truthful,' Matthew says. 'It simply means one group of people presenting something to another.'

Defiant, I run through the list of potential spanners in the works of creating some idealised production: the daylight, the exposing stage, the combination of seated and standing audience members. Does Matthew feel on any level that there is a compromise in being asked to develop a production with so many outside considerations? 'No,' he says. The bear trap twists my leg off. 'It's my *job*!'

The Creative Team ➡

Matthew's close collaborators on *Troilus and Cressida* are the designer Anna Fleischle, choreographer Aline David and composer Olly Fox. As a unit, their job is to find and then deliver a vocabulary that is dramatically effective and helps the audience understand the play.

Before he makes any decisions about the production, Matthew meets the team to discuss the play. He does this as early as possible into the process. The team meets regularly to share research and for Matthew to explain any fundamental shifts in his thinking.

I meet the team a week before rehearsals begin, in a large room at the Globe. By now, the production has a rough shape, but many 'what ifs' remain. Matthew chairs the meeting, and describes successive ideas – images, character insights – preceding many with the disclaimer that they 'might be shit', although this is not an apology. Whilst over half of the ideas discussed today will not survive to the production (some won't make it as far as the rehearsal room), every fragment is a step towards a more elegant solution, and merits discussion.

To 'drag the experience of the play closer to home', Matthew frames the characters of the play in terms of modern events. The Myrmidons, Achilles' private army, will be child soldiers, and Helen of Troy will be modelled on 'vacuous, coked-up' footballers' wives (after all, what is Helen, if not the first trophy wife?).The Greek camp will be informed by trench warfare: like the soldiers of 1914, whose generals expected the war to be over by Christmas, the Greeks live in a 'ramshackle city' that has sprawled with each year of the war from the original temporary camp. A trench will be dug into the stage and, if the theatre allows it, actors will ferry baskets of chickens through bustling crowd scenes. 'And goats,' Matthew adds. 'I asked for goats. I won't get them, but you can always ask.'

After an hour, Matthew has to leave for a meeting elsewhere in the building. Before he goes, he encourages the team to swap phone numbers. 'Feel free to meet if you want to talk about things,' he says. 'I don't need to be there.'

The Script →

The script for the production cuts Shakespeare's text by roughly twenty-five per cent. Matthew cuts instances of 'poetic digression' along with particularly archaic sentence constructions and words ('fraughtage' becomes 'freightage', for example) and references that presuppose a detailed knowledge of mythology. For example, Nestor's command:

> Let the ruffin Boreas once enrage / The gentle Thetis

is redrawn as:

> Let the north wind once enrage / The gentle ocean

To help the audience keep up with so many characters, some of the pronouns – he/she – are replaced with the characters' names.

For some directors – not to mention critics and audience members – to change one word of a text is to commit an unforgivable transgression. Once a writer has died, they argue, the script should be left alone. 'Yeah, I don't understand that attitude,' Matthew says when I put the argument to him. He continues:

> A director would think nothing of asking a living writer to, say, move a line four lines up because the actor who says it has been stood around for ten minutes doing nothing and his story is dying. Why should it be any different if the writer is dead?

The First Day of Rehearsals ⟶

The entire staff of the Globe is present and, when the room settles, Dominic Dromgoole makes an introductory speech. He welcomes the company as guests in his home and recalls his production of *Troilus and Cressida* for the Oxford Stage Company nine years before, and how elements of the play 'outfoxed' him. They still do, he says.

The room clears of all but the company. The designer, Anna Fleischle, places the set model on a table at the front of the room. Floor-to-ceiling, the stage is covered in what resembles marble and dust sheets. The playing area is mostly sparse: a map of Troy hangs over the stage to represent the Greek camp; Priam's palace is represented only by his throne.

The armies will be colour-coded: the Greeks in purple; the Trojans in blue. Celtic body art will tell the story of warriors whose scars are celebrated, for whom each victory is etched into the skin. Matthew warns that 'the white boys are going to get spray tans'. A few of the white boys laugh until they realise he's not joking.

Creating the Prologue ⟶

Rehearsals begin proper with a session from the production's fight director, Kevin McCurdy. The physical language of the play is battle and so, for two hours, Kevin teaches the baby-steps of using swords onstage. He starts slow with choreographed steps, each actor in their own space. Time and again he tells them to 'go slower, slower; slower is better'.

When the basics have seeped into the actors' musculature, Matthew moves the company on to the production's opening sequence, which will be a physical sequence that introduces both sides of the conflict and shows how seven years of conflict, which began in fury, fizzled into cold war.

A solitary drum beats a rhythm, slow and steady. The Greek army enters first and advances towards the audience, stabbing the air in a ritualised incantation of battle. Matthew and Kevin work as a team, developing the sequence in an ongoing cycle of revision. The director knows the effect he wants, and relies on the fight director's expertise to translate his ideas into choreography and refine them with the actors. Matthew will ask for a change of intention or intensity, or for a moment to be punctuated, and Kevin will find a solution. Matthew will suggest a tweak to that solution, and so on.

Paul Hunter is to speak the Prologue. He will do so as Thersites, rather than as the character Shakespeare names 'The Prologue', and this imbues Thersites with an otherworldly quality that the production will go on to explore. Paul speaks the text at first with the patter of a TV reporter, oblivious to the war going on around him. The scene resets and he tries the opposite, weaving among the fighters and ducking their swords, trying not to get killed.

The Trojans enter next, stalking the Greeks, who turn and attack. The battle is fierce. Men bite and claw if it means survival. Gradually, the soldiers tire and stop fighting altogether. A stalemate takes hold. This is the condition in which the play begins.

When the first day ends, at six p.m., the company understands how *Troilus and Cressida* will look and feel, and what the production intends to achieve. An evening beer earned, everyone retires to the pub.

Circuit Training ➡

For the first two weeks, the cast works as a unit. The hours are not always long, but they are well-used. 'We'll work until I've had enough,' Matthew says. 'That might be four o'clock; it might be six.'

The cast assembles each morning at nine, an hour earlier than most productions start work, to run through forty-five minutes of physical exercise, including jogging, yoga, and a training circuit borrowed from the British Army. The play is grounded in war, and physical exercise is, for its characters, 'a means of expression,' Matthew says:

> Working out is a curious way into the physicality of soldiers. It also helps us, as a company, generate momentum to carry us through the day. By ten o'clock, we've already achieved something as a unit.

Reading the Text ➡

Each morning, after circuit training, the company sits to read and analyse the text, decoding each archaic word and unpacking each image. The process is thorough, progressing scene by scene for the better part of two weeks, which amounts to forty hours of discussion for two-and-a-half hours of story.

Poetry, Matthew believes, takes care of itself when its meaning is clear to the speaker, and so he questions the text relentlessly, and he encourages others to do the same. Any answers to a play will lie in its text, Matthew says; not in secondary research nor in details of the playwright's life. 'To go into a text, you have to grapple first with its surface.' He announces this one morning to the company, and I am suddenly aware of how many in the cast have copies of Chaucer's or Homer's versions of the story stashed under their chairs, or unedited copies of the Shakespeare, or academic works about Ancient Greece. All that sits under Matthew's chair is a bottle of water.

'This is our text,' he says, pressing his fingers against his copy of the rehearsal script one day when conversation wanders for the third time towards versions of the story that Shakespeare didn't write. The issue is whether Helen left Greece by choice, or whether Paris kidnapped her, a question that Shakespeare does not address. When someone suggests using Homer's *Iliad* to 'fill in the blanks', Matthew cuts the discussion short:

> Any information that's of use to us will be in our text, which is not the *Iliad*. I agree it's an interesting book and that makes it tempting to use, but that doesn't mean that it will help us understand what Shakespeare is asking of us. His characters might share the same names as Homer's, but they're different people.

In the room, he is calm and teacherly. After hours, he is more blunt on the point:

> Our job is to tell stories written by playwrights, so I question the value of anything that takes us further from those words. I find it immensely tiring when actors keep going back to the *Iliad*. *Troilus and Cressida* is a fiction based on a fiction based on a fiction, so it's nonsense to want to keep referring to anything other than what's in our hands. But, for some actors, things can never be complicated enough. I have even encountered actors who, when you ask them to do something that is written in the script, get out a history book, point at a page and say, 'My character wouldn't do that.' I say: 'Why do you think that book is of any use to you?'

For similar reasons, Matthew places little value in improvisation as a means of developing character. Rehearsals for *Troilus and Cressida* are conducted 'in the present tense', which is to say that the principal vehicle for understanding characters is present action: the things they say and the things they do. As an actor, Matthew has participated in rehearsal processes grounded in improvisation, such as devising lengthy backstories. Whilst he found some of the tasks intellectually stimulating, the weight of creating memories and amassing research 'burdened' him in performance.

It sounds simple: to deliver a compelling performance, an actor needs to know who her character is, and understand the words her character says. But skilled actors can use their craft to try to paper over the gaps in their understanding. Audiences can 'sniff out that kind of fuzziness,' Matthew says. When he suspects that an actor doesn't understand what they are saying, he will ask them to prove that they do by paraphrasing the offending section of the text.

One day, having read the same scene three times, Chris Colquhoun, who plays Hector, is no clearer on why his character makes a detailed and impassioned argument for Helen to be returned to the Greeks, only to reverse himself a few lines later and ask Priam to keep Helen in Troy. Chris shakes his head and turns the script over in his hands as though the answer might be written small in a margin or on the reverse side of the paper. 'Hector just flips. It's inconsistent and I don't think he'd do it.' Matthew nods sympathetically. 'But he does do it. The words are right there on the page, so let's try again to find the reason.'

Within two days, a few actors are twitching in their seats. Frustrated with talk, they want to find a way into the play that uses not only their intellects, but their bodies. Matthew has some sympathy for this. He felt the same way years ago, when the director Richard Wilson introduced him, as an actor, to a reading process similar to the one he now uses. One day, Matthew found the courage to ask his director if the cast could get on their feet. Richard Wilson replied, 'How can you move until you know who you are?' 'That blew my mind,' Matthew says. 'It helped me realise that directing isn't about playing loads of games or doing lots of improvisations, which don't necessarily help actors. Directing is about detail, and detail is about craft.'

The process can be tiring. Matthew brings acute concentration to the room and demands it in return. Some actors feel cross-examined. One says that some days he feels as though he is back at school, drying up for fear of giving a wrong answer. But the results are tangible. Each day, the performances gain clarity and feel less 'acted'. The play's better-known passages, which, being Shakespeare, can so easily feel like self-contained 'greatest hits', grow sharp edges and begin to resonate as immediate thoughts.

Week Two ➡

During the second week, Matthew starts to break up the reading process with exercises designed to help the company assemble the world in which the story takes place.

Three words on theme

The actors write down three separate words that to them sum up the play's themes. The words are then read aloud.

No two answers are the same. For some, the play is about love and honour; for others, betrayal and disorder. The company discusses its differences of opinion and negotiates towards a shared understanding.

Trust

The actors ascribe every other character a number between one and ten that stands for how well their character knows and trusts them.

The disparity tells us a lot about allegiances. Soldier A sees Soldier B as a confidant, but Soldier B sees A as a hanger-on; Soldier C would seek out Soldier D on the battlefield for support, but Soldier D considers C a liability. Most of the numbers are under five: it becomes clear how few allies the actors feel their characters enjoy.

Character ages

The actors ascribe their characters' ages and line up in age order.

As with the exercise above, asking the actors to articulate their instincts helps put everyone on the same page.

Modern items

The actors think of one modern item that their character might carry with them. They are not to censor or reject their instincts unless they are thinking of an object that would dilute the sense of an isolated world, such as a mobile phone.

The answers suggest how the actors are thinking of their characters at this early stage. Fraser James, playing Aeneas, imagines his character going into battle with dance music pumping into his ears from an iPod; John Stahl's Nestor carries a steady supply of beta blockers to calm his nerves; Jay Taylor cannot imagine his character Diomedes leaving home without his toothbrush; Matthew Flynn envisages Agamemnon whiling away the evenings with the board game, Risk; Seamus O'Neill believes that Priam would carry a peace treaty with him in the hope that the war might end today; Paul Hunter describes a pack of butter that Thersites might carry around to eat and to rub on his sores.

Hector's armour

The character Cassandra has the gift of prophecy, but is cursed that her prophecies are never believed. In Act 5, Cassandra is arrested by a vision of Hector dying on the battlefield. Matthew will direct this by having Cassandra, played by Ania Sowinski, trying to purge the image from her head by 'drawing' it with Hector's armour. The cast divides into three groups, each creating a wordless story in which armour and weapons will create a body that the actors will react to. The story is to have three stages: a battle in which the body falls; the moment the body is discovered; and the removal of the body from the field.

Matthew watches each group. He notes how the actors give meaning to inert objects and how their focus draws the audience's eye. This is particularly important given that, as mentioned earlier, the production will not be able to focus artificial light on any part of the stage.

The Final Readthrough ➡️

Before work on the scenes begins proper, there is a final reading exercise. The cast sits in a wide circle. They read the play from beginning to end, with actors who are present in each scene stepping into a second, inner scattering of chairs.

The exercise serves to reintroduce the arc of the whole story, which has faded from view whilst the scenes were studied in miniature. It also rejuvenates the room and highlights where a character is present for a scene but not talking as, for example, is Menelaus for most of Act 1, Scene 3. Richard Hansell, who plays Menelaus, steps into the circle, speaks, then finds himself silent for minutes whilst other characters talk. 'Have I been here all along?'

Putting the Text on its Feet ➔

Nearly two weeks into rehearsal, the chairs are stacked at the side of the room and the company starts to explore the scenes in three dimensions.

For the next few weeks, Matthew will assemble whatever combination of actors he needs for a scene. The company moves between rehearsals, sessions with the production's text advisor, Giles Block, vocal sessions and costume fittings. The rest of the time they find a quiet spot in the theatre to learn their lines, which they have been discouraged to do until now, lest they form associations in isolation from the group.

Matthew rehearses the scenes chronologically, breaking acts into mini-episodes. Work typically begins with the actors reading the text aloud to remind themselves of its shape and to discuss any discoveries they might have made since the reading circle. Matthew describes the geography of the stage, highlighting any scenery that the actors will have to consider, or design elements that will help tell the story. Beyond that, he gives little instruction other than to 'be brave'. The actors must commit to something – anything – and afterwards Matthew will ask questions that inform the next go-around.

Matthew's suggestions usually leave room for interpretation. Rehearsing the scene, late in the play, in which Cassandra (Ania Sowinksi) tries to dissuade her brother from going to the battle that she knows will kill him,

Matthew draws Ania's attention to the tactics she has used, and that, since Hector continues to strap on his armour, she should try something else. She could try to charm him, maybe, or to guilt-trip him. Anything. But the choice must be hers. 'I would never tell an actor how to play a moment,' Matthew explains. 'I might say "That's a massive moment" if I want to remind someone that there's further to go, but I'll let the individual be the judge of what that means.'

Generally, Matthew's preference is for the uncluttered, both in movement and intention. 'When actors move, they should move with commitment,' he explains. 'They must never twitch or wander around. Their intention must be clear.' The actors find their target – which is usually another actor – say their line and respond live to what comes back.

He rarely uses blocking, which is the planning of actors' movement onstage to help the audience understand the story, or to weave subconscious themes and associations under the action. However, when a character receives important information, Matthew often asks that the actor place herself such that the audience can see her face. This could be a question someone asks ('Will you be true?' Cressida asks Troilus before she is traded for the Greek prisoner Antenor) or an answer they receive, such as Hector's non-verbal response – in Act 2, Scene 2 – to the assertion that any man who dies in defence of Helen will not have a 'death unfam'd'. To see the character receive information 'pulls the audience in,' Matthew explains. A thought that the audience cannot see may as well not have happened.

Blocking can also affect how the audience interprets the text. In Act 1, Scene 3, the Greek general Agamemnon assembles his war council. The scene begins with the soldiers standing to attention. After the first rehearsals, the performances are sharp and the stakes are high, but the scene doesn't feel right. Matthew runs through a list of what the scene is supposed to achieve: to establish that the rule of law has broken down, that the soldiers disagree on whether they should remain in Troy, and that Agamemnon's authority is crumbling. And that's the problem: the scene is about the task of restoring order from chaos, but the audience is looking at four people stood in line, waiting for permission to speak.

Matthew restages the opening. The line is broken. The characters walk about the stage, psyching themselves up for an argument. Agamemnon enters, and they pounce, competing over who gets to speak first. That small change, which affects less than thirty seconds of the scene directly, ripples through the next ten minutes.

Matthew is tough on actors' habits. He has worked as an actor himself and considers directing the harder of the two jobs, if only because directors shoulder the responsibility for the piece as a whole. 'I take responsibility for everything that happens in my rehearsal room, good or bad.' To accept this should unleash an actor's creativity, he reasons, as it grants the actor a unique privilege to unburden and play in a house of the director's design. When an actor passes up that opportunity, usually by asking for an instruction right at the start, he gets annoyed. When an actor starts to repeat too readily an action they chose early in rehearsals, Matthew will ask them to check whether they are sure that their choice is 'right' or merely 'easy'.

Working with Actors ➡

Some actors build their performance in slow, sensible steps: they 'don't care what they're like on day one,' Matthew says. 'I've always liked that in actors because they'll be in a solid position when we come to performance and I'll be more likely to trust their instincts.' Other actors arrive at their character early in the process. With those actors, the challenge is to 'keep them exploring and testing their instincts whilst noting their early decisions in case you have to come back to them'.

'Often, directing is *redirecting*,' Matthew says. 'The last kind of director I would want to be is the director who "has all the answers", because that means the actors have nothing to add.' An actor might also turn out to be a different type of performer than the director thought, and so he must refocus his aspirations for a particular moment of the production or even an entire role.

In Paul Hunter, Matthew has cast an actor whose background differs markedly from his own. A founder member of Told by an Idiot, a theatre company beloved for its anarchic, physical productions that 'make no attempt to put reality onstage', Paul was invited to play the role of Thersites partly because Matthew didn't know how else to develop the character other than by editing and shaping the constant reinventions of an actor who works 'from a palette of his own idiosyncrasies'.

Paul generates material at an improviser's pace. He reverses course, experiments and discards idea after idea, provoking the more classical actors in the company to hysterics and, once or twice, to exasperation.

Matthew had 'no idea' what that creative relationship would be like. 'It's been incredibly successful so far,' he reflects.

I used to say in interviews that I never really understand a play until the designer's designed it for me. That's not always the case but it's about each discovery taking you further in your understanding of the play. That might sound obvious, but sometimes it comes merely from observing other people's strong decisions.

The Ending ➡️

The final page of the rehearsal script is a holding page for a sequence not yet devised. Instead of Pandarus's speech that ends the play as written, there is a stage direction:

> *We will have an amazing idea for the end with Pandarus that will change people's understanding of theatre – I ain't had the idea yet!!!*

The final scene of a play is where 'everything lands and ties together what we want the production to say,' Matthew said on the first day of rehearsal. 'Until I figure out what Shakespeare is trying to say in that moment, I can't know what I want to say.'

Two weeks into rehearsal, there is much that Matthew doesn't yet know about the production and he expresses that openly. He even takes pleasure in reversing his position, once unshakeable, that the play isn't funny. 'It's brilliant, isn't it?' he says one evening after rehearsal. 'I was completely wrong – and that's the joy of the process: each stage furthers your understanding.'

He delivers the extra script page at the end of the second week. In place of the monologue, Pandarus is to speak a jarring series of callbacks, his mind now addled by syphilis, repeating fragments of his advice to the lovers and a warning that the world will soon end in fire. Matthew Kelly, who plays Pandarus, will retrace the geography of previous scenes and rail against the space where the characters once stood. He will threaten to leave, and realise that he has nowhere to go.

Towards the end of the speech, Aeneas and Paris will enter with drums. They will advance downstage, beating a steady, military rhythm under the monologue. The entire cast will follow, each with his own drum, and the noise will grow until Pandarus is consumed. The old man forgotten, the world will move on.

The music department delivers the twenty drums Matthew needs to achieve this effect, and as the company makes that deafening sound for the first time, I appreciate the benefit of abandoning recorded sound and focused light. The finale is handmade but unquestionably modern, a lo-fi wall of noise that feeds on itself until the world is filled with sound and fury.

The Jig ➡

Performances at the first Globe Theatre ended with a folk dance known as a 'jig'. Historical details are sketchy – there is no 'jig manual', record of steps or sheet music – but we know that its purpose was to cleanse the theatre, lifting the 'spell' of drama and returning the audience and players to the real world. The jig might parody the story enacted, unite sworn enemies in dance or simply add a note of spectacle to the evening's performance.

Productions at the modern Globe also end with a jig. Depending on its execution, this can register as an afterthought or as integral to the performance.

Two weeks into rehearsal, Matthew is struggling to devise a jig that has a purpose beyond historical curiosity, which is of no interest on its own. He reasons that, whilst it was important for directors of early productions at the reconstructed Globe to ask those fundamental questions about what an Elizabethan-styled building might mean in modern London, eleven years have since passed. Have those questions not been explored? Why should the next generation not be allowed to decide which of the old rituals to use and which to let slide into history? I ask whether he would junk the whole thing if he could, and end on the traditional curtain call. 'It's a big ask, isn't it?' he says. 'To cleanse a space? I don't want to spend two hours telling a tragic story only to undermine it.'

Matthew resolves to go back to first principles. He starts with the notion of a cleansing ritual, then looks at its modern equivalents, from folk dances to the musical numbers that close Bollywood movies. His solution, delivered a few days later, uses the drums from the final scene. Together, actor and audience will purge the story with an uptempo, pounding composition by Olly Fox that combines the production's military aesthetic with dance music and lifts the spell, channelling the audience's euphoria up into the air and out over London.

The First Runthrough ➡️

At the end of the third week, the company runs the play for the first time. Putting the scenes back in sequence and running the production at full speed, the company will be able to refocus and take stock of what they have made so far.

The run will introduce many elements, including Olly's complete musical score, which he will give from an upright piano. 'Just get through it,' Matthew encourages. 'Enjoy getting things right and don't worry about what you get wrong. Anything better than shit will be nice.'

This pep-talk conceals a tactic. Actors who worry about what just went wrong are liable to get more wrong. By inviting the actors to 'enjoy getting things right', Matthew is reminding them that there is a 'right', which is the production that the company has created so far by agreement. 'I'm not saying that the production won't change,' Matthew clarifies. 'But at this stage the actors should trust what we've made together and focus on putting those decisions together.'

Olly sits at the piano, Matthew asks for ten seconds of silence and the run begins.

Two-and-a-half hours later, Matthew is giving notes. He starts with the small things: the mistimed cues, swallowed lines and moments of 'fuzziness'. His notes are succinct and practical ('We listen more to seven notes than seventy'). He makes a suggestion, gives the actor a moment to digest it, and moves on. He questions why Paul Stocker, who plays Troilus, hesitated during a speech, intuiting that he dismissed an impulse. 'I wanted to get on my knees,' Paul explains, 'but I remembered that Agamemnon did the same thing in the last scene and I didn't want to be boring.' Matthew makes a note to return to the scene. 'That intention is important. We need to find something there if you're denying an impulse.'

Act 5 warrants particular attention. As the story propels towards battle sequences, the scenes become shorter and more physical. A few performances are running 'hot', which means that the actors' emotions are running away with their performances, and between the testosterone and the complex fight choreography, the text is in danger of being lost. Matthew highlights the problem and asks the company to take a moment to remind themselves of the stories they are responsible for telling.

One week remains before the company will move into the theatre. Having restored the scenes to their order, the company will disassemble the play again and work on an act each day. Monday, Tuesday and Wednesday morning, they will rehearse scenes and strings of scenes in an act; that afternoon, they will run the act. Thursday and Friday will end with a run of the whole production. By Friday evening, everyone is itching to get into the theatre.

Tech Week ➡

The process of transferring a production from the rehearsal room to the stage is long and complicated, even without having to worry about light and recorded sound. It is also often boring, at least for the actors, whom Matthew warns to expect days of waiting around. Over the weekend, the stage-management team works with the designer, Anna Fleischle, to transform the Globe into Troy. Monday morning, as the cast change into their costumes for the Prologue, the last item of scenery is hoisted into place.

We walk to the stage. A door, painted in magnolia, separates the twenty-first century world, with its sofas and coffee machines, from the wooden beams and thatch of the auditorium, which fills our peripheral vision as we step on to the stage: three storeys of seats stare at us across a yard that holds seven hundred 'groundlings'. Dominic Dromgoole's words replay in my head: 'You have to tell big stories here… big lungs, big action, big thought.'

Within minutes, Matthew is subsumed by questions, which come from every direction: 'Is this haircut okay?', 'Would you like music here?' These will continue until work stops twelve hours later, and resume each morning. With four-and-a-half days to work through the production, he becomes more authoritarian than he was in the rehearsal room. He stops referring to 'the theatre' and starts referring to 'my theatre', and is liable to snap when his questions aren't answered quickly enough, or if an actor makes the same mistake twice. Before, he was first among equals; now he is a surgeon and everyone else is his support team – highly skilled but in his service: this person needs to be *there*, or this item needs to be *here*, and it needs to have happened ten seconds ago.

The acceleration unsettles all but the veterans in the cast. Keen to appease, actors offer assurances that any mistake will not happen again. This is not helpful when it means that people, afraid of upsetting their director, start to dash backstage and miss their entrances. Rehearsing a scene change, the music runs out and the stage is left empty for five seconds before the actor appears, apologising profusely and promising that the journey will be quicker 'on the day'. Matthew prods further: it is one thing for an actor to lose focus for a moment, but it is another matter entirely when there is good reason for a slip-up, such as the difficulty of negotiating a steep flight of stairs in sandals and a long dress.

Music cues are shortened, doubled and doubled again to accommodate actors' journeys backstage or through the audience. The composer, Olly Fox, knew from experience that this would be the case and wrote many of the cues, as four- or eight-bar phrases that can be extended or shortened quickly.

The third day, there is torrential rain. Matthew directs from the seats across the yard. The rain thuds on the ground and on wood, and the acoustics become dull and heavy. Over lunch, Matthew recalls that last year, *The Frontline* played its press night in these conditions. He and Olly arrived that night sure that the evening was ruined, he says. Almost half the audience at the Globe are the groundlings, who are exposed to rain. But what happened next has stayed with Matthew as a reminder of what is exciting about live theatre, and about the Globe in particular.

> Part of the set was a walkway that extended from the stage, deep into the yard. Usually, when it rains at the Globe, actors do their best to stay onstage but, a few minutes into the performance, one of the actors walked down the walkway, into the rain. She was soaked immediately. She looked up at the sky and she sang the first line of her song, which was 'Jesus gave me water', and the audience *erupted*. It was as though everyone had agreed that the rain didn't matter; that an event was occurring and we were all going to be a part of it. I love that about the Globe: it's so uncontrolled. These days, everyone talks about 'event theatre'. Here, you get the event for free.

Dress Rehearsal ➡

Thursday afternoon, the company runs the play for the last time before the first preview performance. In the minutes before, the stage-management team rehearses Hector's death, which requires split-second timing between the actors onstage, and a pyrotechnic effect triggered from offstage.

Hector dies having survived the first day of battle. Pulsing with the adrenaline of victory and of having defied Cassandra's prophecy, Hector gets careless. He sees a man wearing impressive armour that he decides he wants for himself. The man, described by Shakespeare only as 'one in armour', is here a knight clad in black, his face obscured: an incarnation of death itself. The black knight extends a finger and beckons Hector to follow. Hector dares him: 'Fly on. I'll hunt thee for thy hide.' After a short comic scene with Thersites, Hector re-enters, holding the knight's bloodstained armour. He disarms, his sword having finally had its 'fill of death', and kneels by a stream, where he splashes his face and rinses away the events of the day.

At first, he doesn't see Achilles enter behind him with his henchmen, the Myrmidons (here, the child soldiers). Hector turns, and knows immediately that he is out-numbered and too far from his weapons. He begs Achilles to 'forego this vantage'. Suddenly, we realise that Achilles is carrying something under his arm that we didn't notice before. Something wrapped in cloth. He passes the bundle down the line to the boy nearest Hector, who unwraps it. Music starts to rumble. Inside is a modern machine gun. We hear Hector's wife Andromache's voice on the wind. She sings a sorrowful song. The boy looks to Achilles, hesitant to follow his master's orders. Achilles roars for the boy to 'strike' and so he raises the gun. Andromache's voice comes again as the music swells, awful and discordant. She bids Hector 'sleep my baby, sleep', and the boy fires. The bullet passes clean through Hector's eye and he falls, immediately dead.

A pyrotechnic, rigged underneath the stage, will voice the gunshot. When each department is ready, the stage clears of all but the actors. They play the preceding thirty seconds of the scene. The music swells, the boy fires and Chris (Hector) recoils. Only the pyro doesn't fire. The rehearsal stops, then ten seconds later the pyro fires of its own accord. There is no time to reset. The crew can only reiterate the timing and move on.

The dress run begins. Paul Hunter arrives onstage. He now has latex boils on his face and skin painted a sickly grey. He welcomes the imaginary audience with an elaborate bow, which he has not done before, still playing, even at this stage. Throughout the run, he delivers lines from new positions onstage and improvises with props he hasn't seen before.

Ben Bishop, who plays Paris, has been absent for the past two days for the birth of his first child. Back for the dress rehearsal, he adapts quickly, although he has not rehearsed Paris's sword fight with Richard Hansell's Menelaus for over a week. As exciting as it would be to see the adulterer take on the cuckold, the sequence is fatally under-rehearsed and there is no time left. Matthew marks it to be cut.

After the run, the company assembles for notes. The actors walk back through the building, tense and excited. As we reach the rehearsal room, Laura Pyper, who plays Cressida, asks me if the dress rehearsal was 'okay'. I say it was and she lets a little of the tension out from her shoulders. 'So you don't think we're going to get a bollocking?'

A huge portrait of Shakespeare hangs on the wall of Rehearsal Room Three and, as we form a circle, I wonder how anyone gets any work done with the Big Guy staring down at them. Matthew jumps straight into notes. 'I'd love to ask how it went,' he says, but 'we haven't got time. In the interests of economy, I'm only going to go through what didn't work. If I don't mention something, that means I thought it was fantastic.' His notes are mostly practical – stand *here*; don't stand *there*; remember to do *X* – and, importantly, they are reassuring. Ninety minutes before the first preview is no time to destabilise the company. 'You know what you're doing,' he says as he closes his notebook. 'Now go and do it.'

Ninety minutes later, the company of *Troilus and Cressida* gives its first performance.

Troilus and Cressida in Performance ➡

We are sitting in the office at the Globe, an hour before the fifth preview of seven and a few days before press night.

The first preview was 'depressing', Matthew says:

> We put a lot of work into editing the text to prioritise clarity and story. The first preview brought me back to what all our reactions were when we first read the text together six weeks ago. If the production is clear, it will be funny and moving and heroic and exciting. It still needs to be clearer.

Just as the actor in rehearsal relies on the director to tell him how his performance might be differing in practice from how he intends it, a director in preview needs a week's worth of audiences to help him tighten and refocus the work. Although he accepts this, Matthew is 'sort of devastated' when he sees the director Deborah Bruce in the audience of the first preview. 'What did you say to her?' I ask. 'I went up to her at the interval and threatened to come to one of *her* previews':

> When someone you respect comes to one of your previews, you should take the opportunity to talk to them, but the day after. What Deborah said – and you'd think it would be obvious given all the work I've done with the designer – was that it's extraordinary how many times we change the space. She helped me realise how intrinsic the design is to this question of clarity, so I watched the next preview keeping in mind where the picture changes, and that led to a few tweaks.

After the preview, the anachronism of Hector's death was replaced with something of the period: the killer slitting Hector's throat. The gun was a bold choice, but it had to go, Matthew says. The audience never recovered from the shock:

> The moment of Hector's death should be, first, about that loss and, second, communicating that Achilles' reputation is built on cheating. Some people found the manner of Hector's death so extraordinary that they weren't grieving. If ten per cent of the audience laughs – whether it's from the shock of seeing the gun or being startled at the sound – then you've destabilised the environment in which you're trying to tell the story.

Press night

As press night approaches, Matthew feels his role in the production shrinking. Yesterday he watched the show from extreme stage-left. He had a few practical notes to help the actors send the show to areas where he felt it was getting lost. 'Other than that, I'm losing interest,' he says. 'It's time to move on.'

Earlier in his career, Matthew struggled to walk away from a production, obsessing over performances 'beat by beat'. Now, he pushes the actors to maintain the details that he feels are critical to the story, but he is excited to see the production grow from the dead centre of what was agreed in rehearsal. I ask him what changed. 'Experience,' he says. 'And trust. Both of myself and actors.'

That evening, Matthew's notes before the performance are brief. He warns the actors not to let their adrenalin throw them off-course, or second-guess the work they have done so far by trying to see the show through a reviewer's eye. 'Other than that, have fun with it.'

Reviews

The critical response to *Troilus and Cressida* is mixed-to-positive. The most favourable notices are from reviewers with less experience of Shakespeare, which 'reveals something about the relationship between reviewers and Shakespeare', Matthew says. Mini-essays about 'problem plays' arrive on cue along with the requisite debates about whether the production is 'too modern' or 'not modern enough'. However, few doubt the production's skill and textual muscularity. Matthew reads the reviews as soon as they're published. He always does and has even changed productions in response when he agrees. 'A good note is a good note,' he says. 'If I read a criticism and I agree and can fix it, I will. It would be ridiculous not to.'

A few days after press night, Matthew receives a letter from an audience member, a veteran of Shakespeare productions at the Royal Shakespeare Company for fifty years, who writes that the production is 'the second-best Shakespeare he'd ever seen'. A day later, he receives an email from someone who asserts that the production is 'all shouting and the director clearly thinks that his ideas are bigger than Shakespeare's'. 'You will always have supporters and detractors,' Matthew says. 'That's the nature of the job – you need to learn to be comfortable with that and just get on with the work.'

An Audience's Director ➡

Most nights during rehearsals, the company drank together at the theatre and Matthew would join. 'We were a proper team,' he says:

> You would find it hard to get in any rehearsal room the energy we had, and we had it because we cast the show

well. Some directors like to break actors. I wouldn't be able to sleep at night. I hate the idea of directing by negative instruction and I always try to point out when people are doing a particularly good job. Someone told me once that you should never go to the pub with actors because, if you've been a dickhead during the day, they will need to get it out of their system. I think: 'Just don't be a dickhead.'

Looking back on the production, an actor from the company tells me that 'Matthew sometimes presents you with animosity. He wants to see if you're going to rise to it or shrivel. He wants you to rise.' I think that's accurate. Matthew sizes people up, starting with first meetings or auditions – he wants to know that an actor can make his own space in the company. He takes little personally, so he assumes you won't. He pushes hard but never harder than he would push himself. Still, the actor who is not keeping the pace can soon start to feel like a wimp. Matthew praises more than he criticises, but it is human nature to dwell more on the criticisms. What he doesn't understand, Matthew will interrogate until he does, be it an idea or an actor, and he has little sympathy for anyone who complains of being picked on. Actors are professionals who have a job to do, he says. 'And it is a job.' Directing is mostly people management, Matthew says, echoing Brian Clough, the famously unsentimental football manager, whose autobiography he considers the greatest book never written about theatre directing. He remains 'amazed' that actors exist who can finish the day and be happy not knowing what they're saying.

> We get to a position of trust very quickly; to a place where someone can try something so bad that I laugh in their face and the great thing is, they laugh as well. I say a lot that something was brilliant so they should be able to take the flip side.

Early in our conversations, Matthew described a meeting he had with Dominic Dromgoole, the Globe's artistic director, to discuss Matthew's edit of the text. Dominic had questioned Matthew's decision to cut heavily from the Prologue. 'You can't cut it! The language is beautiful!' Dominic had said. 'It's *all* beautiful,' Matthew had replied. 'That doesn't mean I want to sit through three fucking hours of it.' When he tells the story, he wears an impish smile; the smile of a boy about to poke a wasp's nest with a stick.

I suspect that Matthew enjoys being an outsider in this middle-class place, the Globe. I suspect that he likes battling the baggage that so often accompanies Shakespeare's work, which admittedly has little to do with Shakespeare the man, who lived, wrote plays and died just like playwrights before him and after. Indeed, to pay respect to Shakespeare's work is to treat it as you would any other playwright's. To do otherwise is to pack his plays, which pulse with life, with mothballs.

I ask Matthew if his work shares a style or sensibility. He doesn't know, he says, although he agrees that a director's 'personal energy' is always manifested in his productions. And what is the quality of that personal energy?

> Everybody gets on with it in one way or another. I'm not necessarily talking about speed or pace, but focus. Everyone works hard.

A director once told Matthew that, when a production of Matthew's is playing at a theatre in which more than one company is resident at any one time, his actors are noticeable by their 'swagger', which they acquire as the weeks go on. 'My swagger,' he says, 'whatever that means', although I think he knows. In the *Troilus* company, I count three people use the word separately about each other.

One word that Matthew doesn't use much is 'artist'. It occurs to me that, in six weeks of conversations, Matthew has described himself using the word perhaps twice and each time, he followed it with a qualification: 'artists, for want of a better word...' This is not to say that he does not take his work seriously. I ask him to what extent his persona in the rehearsal room is something worn, or who he is. 'It's probably both,' he says. 'It's the person I've become.' That person, however, took years to develop:

> When I started directing, I would barely sleep throughout the production process. I would traumatise myself wondering what the actors might think of me and my process, to the extent that I was in a constant, heightened state – I wouldn't sleep, I wouldn't eat. It affected everything, from my work to my life and my relationships. That's no way to live! I was afraid of taking responsibility and I was afraid of failing, although those are probably the same thing. At the core, those are fears about control; about needing to feel you have the answers. It goes against all my instincts of what it means to be a good person – let alone a good manager of people – to let myself be a control freak, but when I did, it marked a transition. The fact is that a home needs rules and somebody has to be responsible for making them and, actually, people want to be led. There's nothing more terrifying than being looked in the eye by an actor who's found you out, but the only way you can be found out is if you're bullshitting. You work with a company too long to get away with it and why would you ever need to? Because – and it took me years to learn this – you can say 'I don't know.' It sounds simple, but it takes confidence and experience to say 'I don't know', and I certainly didn't do it at the beginning. Now I don't care who's in control! I'm happy to walk out of the room and let somebody else get on with it. I love that and it's changed everything about what I do.

When Matthew started acting, people told him that he was an *actor's actor*, he says. 'I think that means that I appeared sedate and appreciative of the craft.' When he started to direct, he gave actors a lot of attention, and so his peers called him an *actor's director*. But as his understanding deepened of the director's driving role in conceiving and delivering a production, he found people referring to him as a *director's director*. More recently, there has been another shift. It happened on the first night of *The Frontline*, he says, when a rain-soaked audience conspired to make an event that was truly special. 'I know now what my job is,' he says, 'and it took coming to the Globe to fully understand it. There is only one kind of director to aspire to be, which is an *audience's director*. I hope I carried that into *Troilus and Cressida*.'

Steve Marmion

Dick Whittington and his Cat

by Joel Horwood,
Morgan Lloyd Malcolm
and Steve Marmion

Lyric Hammersmith

Steve Marmion is artistic director of Soho Theatre. His productions include *Utopia*, *Fit and Proper People*, *Realism* and *Mongrel Island* (Soho Theatre), *Macbeth* (Regent's Park Open Air Theatre), *Edward Gant's Amazing Feats of Loneliness* (Headlong), and the Broadway transfer of Rupert Goold's *Macbeth*.

Steve was an associate director at the RSC from 2006 to 2007, and has worked with the National Theatre, Royal Court, Theatre Royal Plymouth, Theatre Royal Bath, Watford Palace Theatre, Sherman Theatre Cardiff and at the Edinburgh Festival.

'As directors, our job is communication and our currency is the actor and the script. We have the smoke and mirrors of spectacle, yes, but what is more important is learning the skill to get an actor or a writer around that problem or over that hurdle.'

Steve Marmion

→ Paul J. Medford (The Cat)

Dick Whittington and his Cat
by Joel Horwood, Morgan Lloyd Malcolm
and Steve Marmion

Opened at the Lyric Hammersmith, London, on
27 November 2010.

Creative
Conceived and Directed by **Steve Marmion**
Designer **Tom Scutt**
Lighting Designer **David Holmes**
Music **Tom Mills**
Sound Designer **Nick Manning**
Choreographer **Lainie Baird**
Musical Director **Corin Buckeridge**
Associate Director **Daniel Herd**

Cast
Scaramouche **Nathan Byron**
Mr Fitzwarren/The Prince **Kulvinder Ghir**
Alice Fitzwarren **Rosalind James**
King Rat **Simon Kunz**
The Cat **Paul J. Medford**
Sarah the Cook **Shaun Prendergast**
Dick Whittington **Steven Webb**

Bow **The Voice of Stephen Fry**
Bells **The Voice of Alan Davies**

Ensemble **Elizabeth Alabi, Joanna Bateson Hill, Zofzjar Belsham,
Alice Brazil-Burns, Hugo Joss Catton, Eysis Clacken, Christian
Geddes, Tara-Jessica Hollingsworth, Freddie Jacobs, Ellis
McNorthey-Gibbs, Glenn Matthews, Karl Queensborough,
Deanna Rodger, Tatiana Romanova, Sam Thompson** and
Bertie Watkins

A Pantomime Horse

There is an old joke. A veteran actor takes a job in pantomime. One night, as he straps on the back-end of a panto horse, he wonders aloud what happened to his career. A wag replies: 'It's behind you!'

Towards the end of the 1970s, the subsidised theatre all but stopped making pantomimes. For over a hundred years, pantomimes, with their bawdy dames, slop scenes and raucous singalongs, were as much a part of Christmas as turkey dinners and family arguments. But today, they are more likely to be seen in village halls and in thousand-seat commercial playhouses, and little in between.

A love of pantomime is a matter of taste or, depending on who you talk to, *lack* of taste. Disregard for the form runs so high in some circles that the word 'panto' itself has changed its meaning, from a description of a particluar form of theatre, knowable by strict, if baggy, collections of narrative rules and aesthetic principles, to a verb to describe all that might be lazy in a production. An audience might say of an actor who pulled one too many faces that he 'pantoed' his way through a scene.

But for the director Sean Holmes, the word 'panto' speaks of fantastic stories, performed with full hearts for an audience drawn from every corner of the community – old and young, artist and artisan. When Sean took over as artistic director of the Lyric Hammersmith in 2009, he instituted an artistic policy, two of whose commandments are to 'lurch wildly between high art and populism (hopefully achieving both at the same time)' and the call to action: 'Hammersmith and proud.' At the intersection of these commandments, he would place panto. Every Christmas, the Lyric would become a village hall, welcoming the entire community and asking it to be unreservedly joyful and silly in its appreciation.

The Lyric pantomime would also be done with 'a bit of class,' Sean says. The script would be written by young but experienced playwrights, performed by working actors (rather than TV celebrities), and given a 'proper' rehearsal period, rather than the handful of days often afforded to commercial pantomimes.

Football ➡️

Sean entrusted the Lyric pantomime, its first in thirty years, to Steve Marmion, a thirty-two-year-old director who assisted him at the RSC years before, and whose professional mottos are: 'Thou shalt not bore' (inspired by the theatre polymath Anthony Neilson) and 'Thou shalt not leave thy audience feeling stupid.'

Pantomime is to Steve an 'intellectual fascination' that started with a love of football. 'Theatre and football are essentially the same event,' he explains when we first meet. On any given Saturday, thousands of people attend the theatre. They laugh or weep quietly, gripping the arm of the person next to them. Meanwhile, football stadiums are filled by hundreds of thousands of grown men, shouting, crying and singing with abandon as the spontaneous narratives of injury-time goals, or players scoring against their old clubs move them to higher levels of joy or grief. Our rational side knows that this response is absurd, Steve reasons. The football crowd knows that to cry and shout as two teams kick a ball around a rectangle of grass makes no sense. No more than allowing one's self to believe that an actor is the character he pretends to be. In each case, it is the structure of the event that allows us to care, and incites us to join in. The difference between theatre and football, Steve explains, is that often the further you move from sports towards intellectually challenging theatre, the more 'the emotional connection is allowed to diminish, or at least to display itself with reserve'. Steve hasn't the nerve for karaoke, he says, but he'll stand with the 'hairy-arsed Scousers' at Anfield and belt his team's anthem, which happens to be a song from a Rodgers and Hammerstein musical, 'You'll Never Walk Alone'.

What makes otherwise 'level-headed' crowds express their emotions with such abandon at a football match and not at the theatre? 'The simple answer is that the social rules are different,' Steve says. 'The rules of football encourage us to sing and shout. The rules of theatre suggest we don't. Unless it's a panto.'

Eternal Stories ➡

Dick Whittington is the story of a wide-eyed country lad who pursues his fame and fortune to London, a magical city, he has heard, where the streets are paved with gold. Instead, Dick finds the city infested with rats. He finds work at a local bakery run by Mr Fitzwarren, a local curmudgeon. There he meets the bakery's cook, Sarah, and Mr Fitzwarren's daughter, Alice, with whom he falls in love. From there, the plot depends on the teller, although the story has essential ingredients: the bells of St Mary-le-Bow – the famous Bow Bells within whose earshot the true Cockney is born – must call Dick to his destiny as Lord Mayor of London; there must be a voyage by ship that strands the characters in a far-off kingdom where Dick becomes a hero after his cat clears an infestation of rats from the palace of the island's king. The story must end with Dick returning to London with untold riches, whereupon he marries Alice and, as the Bow Bells peal, is appointed Lord Mayor of London.

The story, like all enduring pantomime stories, is an eternal tale of love, power and control. 'Shakespeare in glitter,' Steve says.

> I think we can challenge people on why they want the things they want. In these days of reality TV, more people say that what they want is fame, but fame and riches are not, in themselves, worthy ambitions. To have enough money that you can provide for the people you care about, on the other hand, and to be recognised for having added value to the world, is a wonderful ambition.

If a production can combine that 'politically valuable moral core' with an escapist roller-coaster, then the audience might even listen.

What is Panto? ➡

Ask 'What is theatre?' and we'll be here all day. Even then, we may not agree on a definition. But ask 'What is pantomime?' and the answer is a little easier. We know a pantomime by certain structural and tonal rules, cobbled together over a hundred years, and without which we may have a piece of theatre – we may even have the story of Dick Whittington and his cat – but it won't be the pantomime version of the story. To be the panto version of the story, our production must:

- Be set in a romanticised vision of the local community, celebrated in song by a chorus of townspeople.
- See love triumph and villains redeemed.
- Have its villain enter from stage-left, and its hero from stage-right.
- Feature original songs and parodies of the popular songs of the day, and a singalong with lyrics printed on an enormous song sheet.
- Contain slapstick.
- Revel in double entendre.
- Challenge the audience into call and response with the characters.
- Feature a dame, which is a man in matronly drag who makes risqué jokes and throws sweets into the audience.
- Allow the actors to acknowledge the audience's presence whilst remaining in danger within the story.
- At some point, bring a child from the audience onstage.

Dick Whittington and his Cat will be written by the play-wrights Joel Horwood and Morgan Lloyd Malcolm, with Steve overseeing as deviser and conceiver. Joel, Morgan and Steve begin by tipping each component of the traditional panto onto the floor and examining each in turn, asking whether it is useful, relevant and fun before putting it back in the box.

Some traditions survive, such as the tradition that scenes alternate between those played in front of brightly coloured show-cloths, and those played among elaborate sets that use the full expanse of the stage. Decided upon before the days of flying and automated scenery, this tradition is no longer necessary, but as it can create a hurtling momentum, the team are eager to keep it. Traditions marked for extinction include the convention that the lead boy is played by a female actor, which, the team feels, lessens the drama. Some conventions are given suspended sentences, such as the convention that a child is brought onstage from the audience, which will survive only if the interaction can be made to affect the story, most likely by transforming the participant into the 'adventure consultant' who gives the characters the key to solving a grave problem they have.

Steve works the traditional story into a grid of scenes that he presents to Joel and Morgan. The group revises the grid until they are happy with the plot, then Joel and Morgan draft the script, dividing the scenes between them (sometimes as arbitrarily as even/odd). They rewrite each other's work until there is a full first draft. Steve oversees the overall tempo of the piece and gives notes on each successive draft. He also suggests where space might be left in the script for physical routines and set pieces to be devised with the actors.

Readthrough →

Two weeks before rehearsals begin, the writing team meets to read and discuss the latest draft of the script. Meeting face to face helps discussions flow more freely than they would by email and lessens the fear of a comment being misunderstood. The script is assessed against three criteria:

- *Clarity* – does the script communicate its intention?
- *Motivation* – do the characters have believable reasons for doing the things they do?
- *Tone* – is it 'panto' and will children understand?

The Lyric's artistic associate, Simon Stephens, attends the readthrough. A formidable and multi-award-winning playwright whose plays including *On the Shore of the Wide World* (2005), *Pornography* (2007) and *Punk Rock* (2009), Simon passes Sean Holmes's notes on to the group before the readthrough begins, and stays to listen and offer his own.

To avoid getting too attached to any particular character, Joel, Morgan and Steve alternate the parts with each scene. As they read, they jot notes in the margins of their scripts, stopping to discuss each scene and eliminate the loose threads that hang over from previous drafts. The trio works quickly, cutting and rewording lines, led by the democracy inherent in humour – if a line does not reliably win laughs, it has to go – and aided by the relative freedom from sentimentality that comes with a script assembled by three writers.

Simon Stephens' contribution is the forensic detail with which he examines the logic behind every pratfall and every line (down to whether a joke linking Mayor Boris the First of London to 'bendy stagecoaches' works when the Mayor's real-life counterpart, Boris Johnson, campaigned against bendy buses), and daring the writers to find a more satisfying reason for the Cat to misplace the object that becomes the play's *deus ex machina* than the necessity of losing it for the sake of the story. He also suggests where characters who don't currently share dialogue might have something interesting to say to each other, such as the Cat and Scaramouche, who are each a sidekick to an idiot.

After the readthrough, Steve collates the group's notes. Joel and Morgan divide the responsibility for rewrites between them. The next draft is to clarify the story ('Hit the main points, keep the story on target!' Simon Stephens advises) and reinforce the dramatic stakes among the belly-laughs, of which there should be more.

Hurtling ➡

Rehearsals take place at the Lyric Hammersmith. On a Monday morning in November, the room fills with the teenage actors who will form the production's ensemble. Recruited from the ranks of the Lyric Young Company, the theatre's youth project that trains young people at evenings and weekends, and during school holidays, their fresh-faced presence ensures that Hammersmith onstage reflects Hammersmith offstage. 'These guys make the show what it is,' Steve says.

The company assembles to read the latest draft of the script. The principal actors sit with Steve at tables in the centre of the room. Everyone else – the writers, theatre staff, the ensemble, Sean Holmes – sits in a wider circle. Tom Mills, the production's composer, sits in the corner of the room, one hand on the volume dial of a PA system, the other on his laptop, ready to play the demo tracks he has recorded for each song. Before the readthrough begins, Steve asks only that the actors try to enjoy themselves and dismiss the voice in their heads that tells them they must entertain the company on their first day.

Ground Rules and Games ➡

After the readthrough, Steve sets the ground rules for rehearsal:

- To be early is to be on time.
- There is a five-pound fine for he whose mobile phone rings in the rehearsal room (fines go into the kitty for drinks on press night).
- As it is a large company, no one is to be offended if, for the first week, anyone forgets a name.

Next, Steve leads two introductory games:

Black box, pink triangle, noisy baby

The company forms a circle. In turn, each person announces their name to the group. They go round again, this time each trying to name the person to their left, then again, naming the person to their right. Then Steve introduces the black box, an imaginary shoebox-sized object. The person who starts with the box says 'Black box to…' then someone's name, and throws the box to that person, who catches it and thanks the thrower by name. And so it goes until the company has worked up a rhythm. Then Steve introduces the pink triangle, which is thrown whilst the box is in play. Last comes the noisy baby, which cries 'Waaaagh!' when you throw it. (Of course, the objects can be anything you like, although it's fun if the last item is silly and noisy.)

Introducing your partner

The cast divides into groups of three, matching two ensemble actors to each principal. Each group is given two minutes to find out something each of them likes, doesn't like and why that person 'likes Dick'. After two minutes, the company regroups and, in turn, actors introduce each other. To watch the company describe why their partner 'likes Dick' is to watch a room of actors struggling to be 'professional' – which is to say, resisting the urge to make the obvious gag whilst their director suppresses a smirk. Eventually, Steve spares the room: he makes the gag himself and the floodgates open.

Warm-up games, especially on the first day of rehearsal, serve two functions. They can be a low-stakes way of getting the company to work together, free from the pressure to impress, and they can engage the imagination, setting the pace for a rehearsal process built on trust and collaboration. Many books have been written dedicated entirely to rehearsal games, and many emerging directors pick from these as if from a shopping list. The skill is choosing the games carefully, using those that fit the purpose, perhaps hinting at the substance of the play itself, or addressing the concerns of a particular company. In the case of *Dick Whittington*, the ages represented in the company vary more widely than most, but the production requires each actor to be bold, to follow their comedy instincts and be willing to fail gloriously in the pursuit of riotous comic turns down the line. And so Steve chooses games that help level the playing field between actors old and young, stacking the dice so that the younger actors, whose egos are more fragile, are likely to win. By asking everyone to make the 'cheap' and obvious joke, Steve is signalling to the company that they needn't be subtle, but should embrace their inner imp.

The Three Rules of Panto ➡

When the company returns from its tea break, Steve is holding up three pieces of A3 paper, on which he has written his Three Rules of Panto:

- *Rule 1* – Baddies enter left; goodies enter right; ensemble enter everywhere.
- *Rule 2* – There will be no 'classy' irony or mini-deaths or subtlety.
- *Rule 3* – What's my motivation? It's a panto.

The Three Rules reinforce the tone of the show. Rule 1 is a pantomime tradition that has practical use in clarifying the story. Rule 2 wards actors away from their first instincts, which will be to psychological realism and deconstructive humour (the 'mini-death' is Steve's term for the embarrassing climb-down that follows a failed joke, which has been the dominant mode of mainstream comedy since *The Office*) and towards panto humour, which is: gag, punchline, repeat. 'No subtlety' refers to humour but also to emotion. 'Say a character does something sentimental. The response is either retching or crying,' Steve clarifies. 'Nothing in between.' Rule 3 clarifies the emotional tone of the show. Panto characters mean what they say and express themselves openly with no ulterior motives or inner conflicts. A hero is a hero. A villain is a villain.

The company breaks for lunch. Before he leaves, Steve pins the Three Rules of Panto on the wall where they will remain, watching over the rehearsal room, until the production moves to the theatre in three weeks' time.

Panic Run ➡

After lunch, Steve announces that the company will run the entire production. There are gasps when Steve announces this, but the lack of preparation is the point.

No one is told where to stand or what to do: the only instruction is to improvise choreography ('Tell the story with your bodies') during the songs, and to join in the call and response (the 'It's behind you' and so on) if you aren't in a scene.

Scripts in hand and eyes shifting between the script and the stage, the actors stumble through the play, grabbing whatever makeshift props make sense to them from the array of objects – cardboard boxes, broom handles – that line the upstage wall, sourced at a moment's notice by the production's deputy stage manager, Caroline Meer.

Despite having been introduced to Panto Rule 2 ('No mini-deaths or subtlety'), the shock of playing the production with no instruction forces most of the actors back to their modern instincts. They pull away from jokes at the last second, and share knowing glances, and joke after joke dies a few feet in front of them, failing to cross even ten feet of air to the audience. But by the second half, the company is adjusting and developing muscle. Actors stop apologising for the jokes and throw themselves into the performance. The audience, seated along the front of the stage, accepts its role immediately and gives rowdy calls and responses.

The exercise gives Steve a 'machine gun' of ideas for later in rehearsal, and allows him to see spontaneous versions of moments that he 'hadn't understood or hadn't solved' before rehearsals. It also removes the fear of 'realising the writer's vision', which can weigh so heavily on British companies conditioned to regard the script as a sacred object and their jobs as realising 'the writer's vision'. 'The most important thing was to take away the fear of telling the story,' Steve explains that evening after the company has gone home. 'I want to turn the script into a plaything.'

Machiavelli ➡

Dick Whittington is essentially a full West End musical, at least in scale. It has a large cast and a live band, but unlike most West End musicals, it has to come together in less than a month. The first week will be 'mayhem', Steve warns at the start of day two. 'This is boot camp. Think of it as three weeks of tech followed by a tech.' He delivers this warning as a dare. 'This is a tall order,' he seems to be saying. 'So let's see how much fun we can have fulfilling it.'

The pantomime world is full of comic sound effects and governed by cartoon physics, and so the rehearsal atmosphere must match its playfulness. The paradox is that spontaneity often requires a lot of setting up. The director must guide without seeming to guide.

'You have to construct a *vibe* for every rehearsal process,' Steve reveals. 'It feels Machiavellian to do so, but it is essential for a production to work.' And so, although he might write detailed rehearsal plans, Steve brings nothing written in the room, memorising the order of the day so that he needn't interrupt the flow of rehearsal or bring the appearance of order to its anarchic spirit. For similar reasons – also to save time in a short rehearsal process – he moves around the room, giving notes quietly to individual actors in the downtime between rehearsal blocks.

The company will find it difficult to perform in the week between Christmas and the New Year, Steve warns: when they are variably hungover from Christmas Day, or resentful that they couldn't drink, or tired from a whistle-stop twenty-four-hour trip to see family. The best way to survive this fatigue is to have created a playful atmosphere in rehearsal that is renewed in performance. The cast laugh in the early days of rehearsal as they remove the in-jokes and adult humour that everyone knew would be cut before performance, such as when Shaun Prendergast's dame, Sarah the Cook, shows off her 'hand-grenade dress' (pull out the pin and it's every man for himself) and, with mock-disappointment, the actors mark lines through their scripts.

Towards the end of the first week, someone brings in flyers for the panto at Hackney Empire. The copy proclaims its production 'London's Number One Pantomime' – and so the Lyric cast set about gleefully defacing their own flyers, adding beneath *Dick Whittington and his Cat* the boast that they are 'London's Number Two Pantomime'.

A Backwards Process ➡

We know pantomime characters from heredity: they are, Steve explains, 'what they say on the tin':

> Dick Whittington is the Dick Whittington you picture when you read the words. The only thing Steven Webb [Dick] wanted to check on day one was: did I want the full-on 'tractor boy' accent, which of course I do.

In this world of archetypes, free from subtext, the actor in panto does not disappear into the role so much as meet it halfway, combining the character's essential qualities with more facets of his own personality than a naturalistic drama would allow. He then 'gags up', which is to say, plays the jokes moment for moment, provided that he stays generous and true to the scene.

Rehearsals for text-based theatre productions often begin with a period in which the company reads and discusses the script to decode its meaning. Here, there is little to unravel. In a psychologically real production, as in life, a person can mean precisely the opposite of what they say. A character in panto almost always means exactly what he says, and so conversations about character are brief; rehearsal usually begins with the actors on their feet, sketching physical business and hunting for the gearshifts in the scene's energy and narrative.

For the first few days, the actors hold on to their scripts as they concentrate on remembering what happens next. Steve keeps his notes brief and practical: a suggestion for a move, a slight emphasis on this or that word. As a rule, he highlights problems only when he can offer solutions.

The scenes are rehearsed largely out of chronological order, in response to whichever combination of actors is available as the company rotates between acting rehearsals, choreography sessions and music calls, sometimes as little as ten minutes on one scene, five minutes on another. One day in the first week, the company picks at three scenes in twenty minutes in response to a rehearsal schedule arranged on the fly.

Still, the production develops quickly and, by the end of the second day, the company is ready to stumble through the first three scenes in full, including a 'production number', which is a term from musical theatre that means a set-piece song with dancing. By the end of the first week, the company has sketched the entire production.

Lucky Generals ➡

Asked how he won so many battles, Napoleon Bonaparte replied 'Lucky generals'. The phrase resonates with Steve, who suggests that a director is strongest when he 'surrounds himself with excellent people and listens to them'. It is this faith that allows four rehearsal rooms to run simultaneously: principal actors with Steve whilst, in the dance studio directly below, Lainie Baird, the choreographer, teaches dance numbers. Dan Herd, the associate director, will accompany Lainie or Steve depending on which rehearsal involves more of the ensemble, or else he rehearses the ensemble separately. Meanwhile, Corin Buckeridge, the musical director, will be working with any number of performers on the musical numbers. Some days, the production resembles a factory running at capacity.

Steve met Dan Herd in 2005 on the Old Vic New Voices 24 Hour Plays. Steve was assigned as Dan's assistant (he was too old to take part) and, on and off, they have worked together since. Their relationship is one of mutually understood nods and sentences half-finished. Directing the ensemble, Dan's role shifts between teacher, big brother and director. For most of the ensemble, this is their first experience of professional theatre, and as they negotiate the steep learning curve between working on a teenager's schedule and working to an adult schedule, Dan is there to push them further and ensure that, later in rehearsal – when they will be expected to get things the second time at the latest – they will be ready. As the associate director, Dan's job is not only to direct the ensemble, but to 'catch the things' that Steve feels he is 'not as alert to'. 'In that sense,' Steve says, 'the partnership is a "divide and conquer". Simply put: my shows are better when Dan works on them.'

Plan B ➡

Rehearsal, Steve says, is 'the search for the most dynamic, interesting, compelling choices'. What vision exists before rehearsal is only Plan B: the provisional version of the show, crafted in detail, but expected to be bettered by the addition of thinking, expert performers. As Steve explains:

> If we end up doing everything that was in my head when we started; if my idea was the best at every crossroad, then there's something very wrong with the people I've chosen to have around me. Beyond the practical considerations, like the fact that the set is already being built, all bets are off. The director should not think 'How do I force you into my vision for a show?', but 'How do you make my vision even better?'

If an actor – or anyone in the room – can top a joke in the script, it goes in. At least once a day, someone tweaks a line or improvises some business that causes Steve to leap from his seat, shout 'You can have that!' and nod to Caroline, the deputy stage manager, to amend the script.

One day, during the break between two runs of a scene, Stevie Webb (Dick) starts to tap dance, using his character's iconic bundle-on-a-stick as a cane. Steve bounds over. 'I didn't know you could tap dance!' Stevie nods. 'Paul (the Cat) can too.' Steve turns to co-writer Morgan Lloyd Malcolm, who is tapping away at her laptop. 'Can you find a place in the story for a tap duo?' he asks. 'Maybe in the final battle against King Rat. We need something to alleviate the violence.' Stevie adds that Ros (Alice Fitzwarren, the love interest) can tap, and Steve turns back to Morgan. 'Then let's make it a trio!'

This pattern of play and revision holds for the first week of rehearsal. Sometimes an actor will ask to rephrase a line that tangled the mouth, or for a new line to bridge the gap between two thoughts that don't yet connect, or feel 'wrong', such as when Alice vents against her father's decision to marry her off to King Rat in the hope of saving the family bakery. Pledging to correct her father's mistakes, Alice says:

> I'm gonna save this business on my own, you just watch, and when I get back we'll deal with all this that's just happened. I am NOT happy, Dad. NOT HAPPY.

What felt proportionate on the page feels aggressive in three-dimensional space. If the writers agree, as Morgan does in this case, she will make the change, which she does here by removing the last two sentences, allowing Alice to be inwardly strong and outwardly soft.

Different Keys for Different Doors ➡

It is a truth universally acknowledged (although not always acted upon) that actors are not talking props. Rather, they are, as Steve puts it, 'artists who have committed their lives to a craft'. Yet the director who respects and communicates well with actors is, he feels, rarer than it should be. Steve recalls the twenty-year-old version of himself who thought he knew everything, who didn't realise how much of the director's job is to look inward and ask 'What can I do to make it easier for actors?':

> The director's job in rehearsal is to enable the actors to be their best within the production you have envisioned, or you envisioned together. Eighty per cent of directing is casting; twenty per cent is *don't fuck it up*. It's about: 'What will unlock this moment or this gag for this person?' You need to give a different type of note to the ensemble than you would to the professional actors, and within the professional actors, each of the six principals take a different approach to their work: some are ex-RSC,

some are West End, some are dancers, some are singers, some are actors. It's constant shifts. With experience, you add more keys to the chain.

With experience and self-reflection, a director learns, too, when to stay quiet, and when to delegate to his generals and how to talk to them. When Steve gives notes to the creative team, he tends to refrain from using jargon, such as when, during a meeting, he asks the production's lighting designer, David Holmes, for 'spinny lights' or asks only that the lighting reflect the 'ominous' or 'weird' atmosphere he wants for a scene: it is for David to invent, and by inventing, to own the solution. 'There is nothing worse than working with a director who wants to "write and sing the theme tune",' Steve says, and for a moment he is talking again to his twenty-year-old self, who didn't know that to direct is to make work 'through collaboration'.

The Storm Scene ➡️

A traditional set piece in the *Dick Whittington* story is a storm that wrecks the boat carrying the principal characters and strands them on a distant and exotic island. The stage directions for this production read as follows:

> *The strobes kick in. The boat breaks up, barrels flying everywhere. Thunder, music, power. Like a 3D film, but in the theatre. Waves keep dunking them underwater. No silks anywhere… A huge surge of water and we enter a brief underwater section where we all sing 'Under the Sea' from* The Little Mermaid. *A massive crash of thunder ends this terrifying (award-winning) scene!!*

The scene calls for 'some full-on primary-school physical theatre,' Steve says. The cast will tell the story of the storm using their bodies, lurching *Star Trek*-style from side to side as they reach for something to grab on to.

The principal characters will then arrange themselves to suggest the bow of the ship whilst the ensemble, in slow motion, run forwards wielding pieces of the ship set, twirling them over the principal characters' heads like cheerleaders' batons to suggest the boat coming to pieces. In the few seconds before the ship flies apart, the Grim Reaper will appear over Sarah the Cook's shoulder.

The scene is a Heath Robinson contraption: it revels in expending enormous physical effort to homespun effect. With the sequence plotted, Steve is jubilant in a way that he hasn't been so far in the process with the actors. The reason is that, before rehearsal, Steve hadn't known how he was going to stage the scene. The solution was 'a combination of three things,' he says that evening. 'Some of it was made up on the spot, some of it I stole from a student piece I directed five years ago, and some of it was Plan B.' He later reflects that the sequence is for him one of the most exciting in the production. 'I want the kids in the ensemble and in the audience to be inspired by what theatre can achieve, and we had slow motion, and the spirit of dance representing anarchy and chaos. It's Complicite on a shoestring!'

Bow and Bells ➡

Part of the spectacle of pantomime is a guest appearance by a celebrity. The celebrity element of *Dick Whittington* will be found in the show's narrators, the anthropomorphic bells of Bow Church, designed by the puppeteer and theatremaker Max Humphries. The plan is that the bells will be voiced by a beloved comedy double act, and so far, numerous combinations have been suggested. First conceived as cartoon Cockneys, the Bells' dynamic has changed many times, from being modelled on various double acts, to, most recently, a version of Statler and Waldorf, the cantankerous Muppets who heckle Kermit and co from the safety of their opera box. Of all the components of the show, Bow and Bells are 'the one that's never sat,' Steve says, mostly because they are an unknown quantity. 'We'll know who they are when we know who's voicing them.'

Three weeks into rehearsal, news arrives that Stephen Fry and Alan Davies have agreed to voice the Bells. This sends Morgan and Joel into three frenzied days of rewrites to adapt the script to Fry and Davies' onscreen personas, particularly their sparring relationship on their TV quiz show *QI*, in which Davies' puppyish energy runs afoul each week of Fry's kindly headmaster.

The Last Week in the Rehearsal Room ➡

Throughout the final week in the rehearsal room, the company revisits scenes, adding layers of detail, and refining the work already done in progressive cycles around the material. Each morning, the company works on individual scenes; each afternoon, they run the 'footdown' version of the show, staying tight on the cues and scaling back any improvisation. Each performance will have its own energy and chaos, but before then, the production must find its baseline.

These final days in the rehearsal room are particularly important, Steve says. 'We are now in the window of time that can make the difference between a good show and a great show. Now is when we can give the production some extra attention.'

So far, Steve has resisted assembling the company and asking them to sit for formal notes sessions, but the time has come and, although Steve never gives notes from behind a table (choosing instead to sit on the floor with the actors), something of the cavalier atmosphere of the process so far is dampened for good.

The actors are starting to tire, both of the schedule and of the material, which they have now delivered so many times that the jokes no longer make each other laugh, or those dotted around the room watching. The danger is that individuals start to reinvent lines or even whole sequences, chasing the intensity of an old high. When this happens, Steve asks the actor to hold their nerve and 'stay honest': what was funny three weeks ago will be funny to an audience who has not seen the show.

The pastoral element of the director's job is coming into sharper focus. As a rule, Steve starts to close rehearsals by asking the company if there are any particular moments in the show that are causing any worry and would benefit from being revisited. To help the young actors stay positive, and keep them alert, Steve asks the group to make notes on each other's performance. Crucially, they are not to tell each other 'where they were shit', but 'where and how they might make their performance better'.

Four Options, Six Previews ➡

On Thursday, the production suffers a setback. 'The second half was awful,' Steve tells the company after it runs the production for the second time that day. 'Something isn't working,' he says, and he is eager to tell the company that, whatever the problem is, 'it isn't any of you'. For the first time in weeks, he seems lost for words. He tries a few explanations, each trailing off into shrugs. 'It's hard to put a finger on,' he says, eventually. 'Thinking hats on everybody; all suggestions welcome.'

Steve and I eat dinner in a pub across the road from the Lyric. Steve eats his meal joylessly, and talks constantly as he works through the problem, which lies with the second half of the story, he says, after King Rat, disguised as a captain, has convinced Mr Fitzwarren that he can pilot a ship carrying Alice, Sarah the Cook and a boatload of Sarah's pastries to sea in search of business. Dick and the Cat, having realised that the captain is King Rat, have stowed away, and suddenly a storm wrecks the ship and the characters wash up on a desert island, Timbuck-three, ruled by a garish Bollywood prince.

Are there too many events in the plot? Should Steve cut a whole scene – perhaps his decision to employ the convention of bringing a child from the audience onstage at such a crucial point in the plot? Should he cut a rousing musical number sung by Dick, the Cat and Sarah to buoy their spirits as they contemplate their situation? (Whilst the song guarantees a singalong, it has little narrative function.)

To solve the problem, Steve considers four different versions of the second half, each omitting an event in the plot. His stress drops a little – fortunately, the maths add up: there are four possible versions and six previews to play with.

The Last Day in the Rehearsal Room ➡

On Friday, the recording of Stephen Fry and Alan Davies as Bow and Bells arrives, having been edited into cues the day before. That afternoon the cast prepare for its tenth run of the show, the last before moving into the theatre the following Monday. Before the run begins, Steve presses the importance of leaving no worry unsaid and no impulse untried before the production leaves the rehearsal room. He dares the company to 'enjoy getting the production right', and earn itself a late start on Monday.

By now, the ensemble is 'on top of the show; no longer chasing after it', which means that the actors are reliably hitting their cues and maintaining their energy throughout the second half. However, complacency has started to set in and the production's running time stretches with improvisation after improvisation. Steve damns the run with faint praise – 'It was solid,' he says, 'a bit comfortable, a bit safe' – although this is good news, as it means that the performers are confident and ready for the next stage of the rehearsal process. As we leave for the day, I suggest to Steve that he must be happy with the production's progress. He nods, and for a moment, he is the Machiavelli of the early part of rehearsals. 'It's calm now,' he says quietly, 'but when we get into tech everything will change and we'll need as much time as possible. Giving the cast a late start on Monday buys us some overtime later.'

The Tech ➡

There are four days until *Dick Whittington* opens to the public. It is Monday morning and the auditorium of the Lyric Hammersmith buzzes with activity. The cast arrive and, as they move to the stalls to hear the mandatory health-and-safety briefing, they notice the Bow Bells, which have been hoisted into place either side of the proscenium in their most elemental form. Today, they are plain wood cut-outs with empty holes for mouths and covered in pencil markings.

Steve begins by managing expectations. He apologises in advance for any lapses in politeness over the coming week, and asks that Row J of the stalls be left clear so that he can run about in the dark and not break a shin or knock over someone's coffee.

The changes begin with the very first image, in which Dick Whittington, asleep in bed and dreaming of London, is seen through a gauze curtain that hangs at the front of the stage. The gauze, it turns out, is more transparent than expected, which means that the ensemble members who hold Dick's bedsheet in place are as brightly lit as Stevie (Dick). The show stops, ten seconds after it started, and the theatre is a flurry of opinions and suggestions. From the lighting desk, David Holmes, the lighting designer, is arguing for refocusing the lights to counteract the transparency of the gauze. Onstage, Stevie is highlighting the fact that the speakers aren't loud enough for him to hear the voice-over narration he's supposed to react to.

It is for these reasons that Steve likens tech to a martial-arts sequence in a Bruce Lee film (his third military analogy after 'boot camp' and 'lucky generals'):

> It's like you're fighting fifteen challenges coming from fifteen different directions. It's question after question after question, so you're constantly making decisions and there's no time to procrastinate. When I first started directing, I would look at my shows during tech and wonder why they didn't look anything like they did in my head. But the job of directing is communication. It took me ten years to accept that, if you look at the show and it's not what you wanted it to be, it's no one's fault but your own.

Safety ➡

There are three days to go of the tech process when the costumes arrive. The production slows down again as actors acclimatise to how the feel of their costumes affects their movement, and how long it takes them to get dressed between scenes – or, in the case of the ensemble, often within scenes. The priority must be safety. The performers can work only when they are not worried about being flattened by lights or tripping over each other in the wings. Within the more complex movement sequences, an actor crossing even a foot further downstage could put him in the path of someone who might be running, jumping or even cartwheeling. Steve instructs the actors to stop the rehearsal if they are, even for a moment, worried about safety:

> There will be things that the actors [onstage and under lights] cannot see. They need to know that I will be listening to them to make their lives easier the moment I have the chance to. In the meantime, I want them to solve problems, not look for more.

A Second Wind ➡

Suspended either side of the proscenium, Bow and Bells are nightmarish versions of themselves. Skeletal and unpainted, their eyebrows wag up and down on thick steel wires.

Below their watch in the auditorium, the combination of early starts and late finishes is taking its toll on the company. Rehearsing a song, Shaun (Sarah the Cook) rolls the drum he is playing offstage and straight into the painted backdrop, which rips. An hour later, rehearsing the storm sequence, a piece of cardboard wave comes unstuck and smashes into the proscenium. It falls to the stage, too light to hurt anyone but causing alarm. Elsewhere, there are a few missed entrances as ensemble members arrive half-dressed in their costumes, still adapting to the quick changes.

The pressure on Steve is building. 'Everyone has to know that Daddy's on top of things,' he says during the morning break, having had to defuse an argument between two actors. 'You have to protect other people,' he says.

> That can be frustrating when other people's spirits are not as generous as yours (or are more generous than yours), but you can't share that frustration with the company very often, because to share would be indiscreet, or it would seem weak.

He takes a minute alone, drinks a coffee and heads back to work. Minutes later, he is sitting in the stalls, calling out the titles of songs he wants the band in the orchestra pit to freestyle. '"Billie Jean"!' 'The Peter Gunn Theme!' 'Do you know any Led Zeppelin?'

The diversion buys the company a second wind until Sean Holmes arrives. As the theatre's artistic director, Sean's role on the eve of the production's first night is to remind the company that they are supported; that they are part of the building. As a stranger to the weeks of rehearsal, he can see afresh and give the company the boost it needs. He thanks the cast for their hard work and reassures them they have an entire preview period before they need to consider the production finished. Before he leaves, he offers one practical note: he points to the back of the upper circle, far above the eye-line of anyone on the stage. 'Throw your first line all the way up there and you'll be fine.'

Wednesday's dress rehearsal will observe the same times as a real performance. The actors will be called to their dressing rooms an hour before curtain, and they will observe the fifteen-minute interval between acts. Steve sits in the dress circle and instructs whoever is near from the production team to sit within 'lashing' distance. Dan Herd, the associate director, cleverly 'mishears' this and sits downstairs.

With one day to go, Steve wears his frustrations on his sleeve, at least with his generals. Watching the run, he sits forwards in his chair and cannot help reaching out for each fractionally mistimed line and technical cue as if reaching to catch an item about to fall from a table. Up here, from the safety of the dress circle, it seems easy: 'Why didn't that actor leave half a second before saying that line?... Why didn't the band come in sooner than that cue?' Onstage, under the lights and powered by adrenaline, it is another story.

After the dress rehearsal, the cast assemble in the stalls. Steve gives notes in a record time: four minutes. 'The good news is that the show doesn't need major surgery,' he says. 'Now let's all go home and have a massive sleep.'

Tomorrow, there will be an audience. Hanging to the side of the proscenium, Bow is complete; resplendent. Bells looks like the exoskeleton of a Terminator.

First Preview ➡

The creative team are first in. Having worked through the night on new ideas for the production, they are optimistic and grumpy in equal measure. Trudging to the theatre café, they prime themselves with caffeine and pink muffins (on sale from today), the Lyric's version of Sarah the Cook's 'super sparkly pinky party pastries'. We plod into the auditorium past ushers loading their merchandising stands with programmes, sweets and glowing toys. A chalkboard by the entrance to the auditorium carries running times for each half based on the dress rehearsal last night.

In the auditorium, Max Humphries, the puppeteer, has finished Bells, whose wise face reminds me of an Old English Sheepdog. Upstairs, Steve and Dan gather the ensemble. Steve is in a mood to grant wishes. 'If I could grant you one wish for the show, what would it be?' he says, then adds quickly, 'It must be something that needs to be solved, and it must be achievable.' Everyone is sure they are content. Steve repeats the offer and emphasises that it is not a trick question. Eventually, someone pipes up. 'Well... I suppose I would be a bit happier if the stairs that lead to the rostra upstage were marked with fluorescent tape, so I could see them better in the dark.' Steve nods. 'Fluorescent tape. Okay. Done. Anyone else?' The floodgates open. 'It hurts my knees when we have to kneel during the storm sequence, so could we have knee pads?' Steve makes another note. 'Kneepads. Yes, you can.' Soon, there are five or so small and simple fixes that the cast agrees on. At the start of a long and intimidating day, everyone feels that bit more secure.

The second dress run takes place as early as possible to allow enough time to look at any 'car crashes' before the evening show. There are none. Steve asks the cast if they are excited about opening the production tonight, or terrified? In unison, the reply comes: 'Both.'

Before going for dinner, the company receives a last round of notes. These are brief: the time between a final dress rehearsal and a first preview is no time to 'go mad with changes,' as Steve puts it. Rather, it is the time for the director to step back and let the company get its bearings. He has one 'killer' note for each principal actor, which he delivers privately in their dressing rooms. He has been sitting on some of these notes for days now, waiting for the time when they will be most effective. For Ros (Alice), it's 'Slow down'; for Sean (Sarah the Cook), it's to remember that the dame, in her role as the show's 'mum', allows the audience to regress, and so should bring the audience into her embrace before she gets bawdy. For Kulvinder (Mr Fitzwarren/The Prince), it's 'Man up', meaning 'Take ownership'; and for Nathan (Scaramouche), it's 'Focus.' 'Simple but effective,' he hopes.

A few hours later, the auditorium is filled by hundreds of children singing along to the pre-show music – sourced from whatever pop music is in the Top Twenty this week – and kicking the seats in front. The final song before the curtain rises will be a Justin Bieber song. 'Watch the kids get inside the music,' Steve predicts. 'They will go mental.'

The audience in a pantomime is the most important character in the show, Steve explains. The response of children in the audience will tell the writers where the story lulls and where a double entendre is only a dirty joke. We soon learn that Rodgers and Hammerstein puns ('Salmon-chanting Evening', *ba-dum*!) sink fast, as do references to Ann Widdecombe and the movie *Jaws*. A gag in the second half, in which the Prince stops the band from playing Coldplay because it's not 'panto', wins an unexpected round of applause, and 'Bad Rodents', a Lady Gaga-inspired production number by King Rat and his crew of rats, is met with cheers.

After the show, Steve gives his briefest notes session yet: 'Congratulations, everyone, we made Christmas happen for four hundred kids. Now: beer.'

Choosing Your Battles ➡

There are eight more previews before press night. The first preview takes place on a Saturday night, and the company, having had Sunday to rest, regroups on Monday morning to work through notes. With every department wanting its contribution to be the best it can be, there is a battle over who gets to use the stage. Steve as King Solomon divides the competing claims into those that can be addressed in time for the next show, and solutions for the long term, such as changes to lighting sequences, which can be implemented gradually until press night on Friday.

The cast first revisits the show's opening number, a parody of Journey's 'Don't Stop Believin'', recently revived in the popular imagination by its inclusion on the TV show *Glee*. The cast is small and looks exposed on the large stage and so Steve assembles the creative team, which approaches the problem from three sides: Lainie revises the choreography to make more use of the stage whilst David refocuses the lights to close down the space. Steve, for his part, adds an 'unashamedly cheap trick': the cast will throw handfuls of silver glitter as the curtain rises. To help the pace, a thirty-second guitar solo is cut along with a large chunk of expository dialogue between the Bow Bells and the Cat.

With the opening sequence ninety seconds shorter and feeling more punchy, Steve moves on to the problem of helping those children in the audience who were quiet during the first preview loosen up in front of their parents and teachers. Steve asks Shaun to tell the kids during his first monologue that, no matter what the adult who brought them says, they must shout.

There are revisions throughout the preview process. Some are minor, such as adding sound effects to clarify transitions and punctuate moments in the storytelling. The Bow Bells' dialogue is cut by a third across the first week, down to its expository minimum, with one strong joke per appearance.

An Old-fashioned Showman ➡

The reviews for *Dick Whittington* are, on the whole, ecstatic. The evening is 'deliriously enjoyable', writes the gentleman from the *Independent*, with 'the right amount of good, clean filth in a witty script... that is even richer in groan-worthy gags and verbal slapstick for the kids'. The review in the *Daily Telegraph* goes as far as decreeing that with *Dick Whittington*, the Lyric has 'knocked Hackney Empire off its pedestal' and found in Shaun Prendergast 'the finest, funniest panto dame in London'.

Steve reads the reviews as they're published. He always does.

> Rightly or wrongly, reviews are the measure of how a show will be judged or remembered by those who were not there. And more often than not, reviewers are right. I don't direct my shows based on what I think they want to see, but I am conscious of their perspectives as I work, just as I'm conscious of my biggest critic, who is my mum. On any show I do, I'll watch one run imagining my mum next to me, imagining what I'd be embarrassed for her to see, or proud to show her. You have to do that: as the director, you must be everyone in the audience.

Steve is, at heart, an old-fashioned showman; a carnival barker. When he describes a past show or pitches an idea, he has a marketer's flair for pitching the *hook* first, whether it's an exciting casting choice or a moment of memorable stagecraft. He lives the motto of one of his mentors Anthony Neilson that what is 'cheap', which is to say spectacular or vulgar, and what is 'serious', which is to say 'high-art', are not opposites, but should be mixed together in a passionate, experiential mix of form, humour and spectacle.

It is his commitment to this idea that allows Steve to ask a cast for silence and concentration, only moments after he has donned the giant monkey-head from the costume box and tried to sneak up on the choreographer. It is a promise made to himself and projected in the work to take the work a little more seriously, and himself a little less so.

Sean Holmes, the Lyric's artistic director, considered directing the pantomime himself before deciding to hire someone else. He told me this when we first met, sitting at the back of the auditorium whilst onstage, actors walked through their vocal exercises for a midweek performance of Sarah Kane's *Blasted*, which Sean directed.

> When you're young, you think you can do it all and so when you don't get a job, you get angry and you want to know why. When you see the eventual production, hopefully, you might realise why the person who got the job beat you to it. Almost always, it's because they could bring something to it that you couldn't.

Steve got the job for a number of reasons, some of which started as far back as childhood, with a boy who read joke books end to end, building a mental encyclopaedia of classic joke structures. Steve started his career teaching and working with youth theatres, so he is comfortable working with children and young adults, and drawing inspiration not only from philosophers and the classical canon, but from Lady Gaga and from 'all of these artists who are offering insight and change and glimpses of what it means to be human'. It would, if nothing else, be foolish to ignore a young audience's reaction to them.

Steve is now artistic director of Soho Theatre. From living a freelancer's lifestyle, his days are managed by an assistant, and more people in his professional life than ever before want to buy him coffee and talk to him. When we meet to catch up a few months after *Dick Whittington*, he bounds downstairs, and we start to walk through Soho. He lights a cigarette and breathes out the combined weight of three meetings so far this morning. We go to a restaurant, a friendly pop-up affair a few streets from the theatre. I ask whether the job so far has given him any insight into directing. 'Yes,' he says and he addresses my dictaphone directly:

> Be yourself. Don't try to make the shows that you think artistic directors want to see. It's really easy to tell when someone's doing that, and if you play that game for long enough, you'll lose sight of what really interests you, so much so that when you have the chance to return to that, it will take you a long time to find your voice again.

Back in Hammersmith, work is already beginning on *Aladdin*, next year's panto at the Lyric, which Steve will direct, fulfilling a three-production contract with the theatre, and collaborating with mostly the same creative team. Just as *Dick Whittington* solved many of the problems of its predecessor, *Jack and the Beanstalk*, *Aladdin* may solve many of *Dick Whittington*'s problems whilst creating a few more of its own. But that's the fun, Steve says. 'Unless a day changes you, even a little bit, I don't see the point in getting out of bed.'

Natalie Abrahami

A Midsummer Night's Dream
by William Shakespeare
Headlong Theatre on tour

Natalie Abrahami is associate artist for Hull Truck and was joint artistic director of the Gate Theatre with Carrie Cracknell from 2007 to 2012. Credits for the Gate include *Yerma* (also Hull Truck), *How To Be An Other Woman*, *The Kreutzer Sonata* (also La MaMa E.T.C.), *Vanya*, *Unbroken*, *The Internationalist* and *Women in Love*. Other theatre includes *After Miss Julie* (Young Vic), *Pericles* (Regent's Park Open Air Theatre), *Guardians* (HighTide), *The Eleventh Capital* (Royal Court), *Play* and *Not I* (BAC) and *Human Rites* (Southwark Playhouse). Natalie was recipient of the James Menzies-Kitchin Award for Directors in 2005.

'I often feel like I'm playing cards – there are fifty-two cards in the pack and fifty-odd ways to play. The fifty-second card reads "This is the way I want this done", but I've never played that card and it's important to me that I don't. I'd rather question and guide.'

Natalie Abrahami

Left to right: Deirdre Mullins (Fairy), Emily Joyce (Titania), the changeling boy (Michael Dylan), Faye Castelow (Fairy) and Christopher Logan (Fairy)

A Midsummer Night's Dream
by William Shakespeare

Opened at the Nuffield Theatre, Southampton, on
3 February 2011.

Creative
Director **Natalie Abrahami**
Designer **Tom Scutt**
Composer and Sound Designer **Tom Mills**
Lighting Designer **David Holmes**
Video Designer **Ian William Galloway**
Casting Director **Joyce Nettles**
Assistant Director **Chris Hill**
Costume Supervisor **Antonia Rudgard**

Cast
Theseus/Oberon **Justin Avoth**
Hippolyta/Titania **Emily Joyce**
Robin Goodfellow/Puck **Sandy Grierson**
Lysander/Snug **Oliver Kieran-Jones**
Demetrius/Snout **Max Bennett**
Hermia **Faye Castelow**
Helena **Deirdre Mullins**
Nick Bottom **Christopher Logan**
Egeus/Peter Quince **David Shaw-Parker**
Flute **Michael Dylan**

How to Start

A young lady, Hermia, wishes to marry. Her father also wishes her to marry, but they disagree on the groom. Hermia loves Lysander; her father wants her to marry Demetrius. In mythical Greece, where the story takes place, the punishment for defying a father is death. Unwilling to acquiesce and unwilling to be put to death, Hermia flees Athens with Lysander, confiding her plans in her friend Helena. But Helena loves Demetrius and she attempts to win him by revealing to him where Lysander and Hermia have escaped to. Demetrius and Helena pursue the lovers to a wood that just happens to be home to a fairy kingdom whose king and queen are experiencing their own trouble in paradise... which is where things get really interesting.

One of the most exciting challenges for a director is to find a new way into a familiar text, and few texts are more familiar than *A Midsummer Night's Dream*, a play that to millions of people conjures memories of those far-off days of school exams, when the teacher would dim the classroom lights and show a beaten-up video-tape of whichever film adaptation cut the least of Shakespeare's text.

Each year, the theatre company Headlong tours a mid-scale production of a Shakespeare play. For 2011, the company settles on *A Midsummer Night's Dream*, drawn to its inherent theatricality and its celebration of the imagination, not to mention its ability to attract audiences compared to other, less accessible plays in the canon.

The production process begins eleven months before rehearsals, with the production's director, Natalie Abrahami, and her designer, Tom Scutt. Separately, Natalie and Tom read the text before meeting to discuss how they might approach a production. Their first attempt – a false start – sets the story in a weather studio and makes heavy use of the film-making technique by which weather forecasters loom in front of computer-generated maps, and which allows superheroes to fly. Called 'chroma keying', it works by filming an actor against a green- or blue-cloth background, which is then swapped out by computer for another image of video. If the subject wears clothes of the same colour as the cloth, then those parts disappear: the arm that operates a puppet, for example. Natalie and Tom's early concept places the human characters in a dreamworld achieved by chroma key, with tiny fairies played by actors in green suits who speak their lines into microphones, and whose transformation is completed by computers.

The aesthetic carries Natalie and Tom for weeks, and ultimately into a meeting with Headlong's artistic director, Rupert Goold, who advises that the concept needs to connect the various worlds of the play rather than focusing on the magical world as a lens through which to see the others. Seduced by an aesthetic, Natalie and Tom had focused on details instead of characters and story. 'The concept must be large enough to lend weight to the whole play and shine new light on it,' Natalie says when we meet in mid-2010, as she and Tom redouble their efforts.

This time, they begin with the motor that drives the story, which is a reality in which a father's power over his daughter is binding to the point of death. Because nothing in contemporary, liberated Western life comes close, Natalie looks for an alternate world that might serve as an analogy for Ancient Greece.

> I thought: what is a duke and duchess in our society? We have a royal family, of course, but their status is much reduced. Who are the equivalents now? It seems that it's footballers or film stars.

She becomes intrigued by the dying days of Hollywood's Golden Age, and in turn by the turn of events in which a major Hollywood studio, Twentieth Century Fox, bet its future on a single picture: a sword-and-sandals epic called *Cleopatra* (1963). The production began shooting without a finished script, and it wrapped years later, having suffered numerous personnel changes and breaks in filming whilst enormous sets, built on overtime rates, sat unused and highly paid actors racked up expense accounts. All told, the production cost twenty times its original budget. For context: adjusted for inflation, *Cleopatra* cost more than Peter Jackson's entire *Lord of the Rings* trilogy.

Even then, it's a lousy film.

Tom and Natalie develop the concept through weeks of coffee-house conversations and design-studio visits.

Natalie focuses on Puck, aka Robin Goodfellow, who is in Shakespeare's text a servant of the fairy king, Oberon. The reference for Puck becomes *Cleopatra*'s director Joseph L. Mankiewicz, who survived making the film by alternating injections of stimulants and sedatives, managing his stars during the day and writing script pages at night. In this production, Robin Goodfellow will be the director of a Hollywood epic, *Where the Wild Thyme Blows*, produced by the Athens Picture Company.

The dream of the play's title is Robin's dream, which he enters late one night after a disastrous day at work. Exhausted by his stars' demands, and depressed that the project is losing its distinctive flavour, Robin pours a large glass of whiskey and turns up the record player. As he reviews the day's footage, his mind wanders. He always seems to have a headache but this evening it's worse. The footage starts to glitch and the sound warps. Suddenly the power cuts. Cables fall from the ceiling and Robin – and the audience – are pulled down the rabbit hole and into the forest, which is the film studio at night; the cracked-mirror world where we discover secrets about ourselves and our relationships. As Robin tries to make sense of these unfamiliar surroundings, a fairy appears wearing blue-red 3D glasses. She releases Robin from the Hollywood studio system, giving him a new name, 'Puck', and releasing him to be the impish storyteller of his dreams. Able to conjure spirits and interfere with time, Puck/Robin Goodfellow creates a story that embraces his imagination and allows him to ruffle the feathers of the stars who torment him.

The tradesmen, Shakespeare's 'mechanicals', will be the production's below-the-line crew, and their performance of *Pyramus and Thisbe*, which closes the play, will be their end-of-production tribute to the film's stars, sweet in its lo-fi clumsiness against the high production values of *Where the Wild Thyme Blows*.

In addition to the fiasco of its production, *Cleopatra* is infamous for introducing to each other its stars Elizabeth

Taylor and Richard Burton. The pair would begin a tempestuous affair on set that would be followed by groupies and paparazzi for years to come.

Natalie conceives Theseus and Hippolyta as Burton and Taylor, composed and electrifying in public, with Oberon and Titania as their volatile private personas. The fairies will be Theseus and Hippolyta's entourage: the geeky, autograph-hunting consumers of cinema, crossed with that invention of the 1960s, the paparazzi. Oberon's entourage will be cowboys who holster their guns in popcorn buckets. Titania's entourage will be gingham-dress-clad groupies. Helena, Hermia and Demetrius will be actors, and Lysander, Demetrius's stunt double. Egeus will not be Hermia's father, but her agent, keen to protect his investment. The characters Philostrate and Starveling will be removed altogether, their dialogue redistributed mostly to Puck.

The concept is bold and intricate. After she explains it, I ask Natalie the question so many ask of companies and directors who reconceive a classical play's setting so fundamentally: if Shakespeare was a genius and if his plays are timeless, then why not produce them uncut, in their original context, in period dress? Natalie takes a long breath as if steeling herself to go over the top of a trench into enemy fire:

> Every time I read a Shakespeare play or watch one of his plays in production, I am reminded how powerfully they speak to us, whether it's the 'Seven Ages of Man', 'What fools these mortals be' or 'Tomorrow and tomorrow and tomorrow'. We ask: 'What does it mean to be human?', and someone replies: 'Read *Hamlet*.' 'What is ambition?' 'Read *Macbeth*.' Shakespeare may have happened to be writing four hundred years ago, but he is writing about now, and his plays are as cogent and as poignant as they were four hundred years ago. However, they can seem impenetrable, so we need to find ways to help us engage.

Of course, dutiful 'archive' productions can be staged, but archive productions won't attract new audiences. To keep an audience engaged, the story must always be a few steps ahead of the audience. Modern audiences might not be so attuned to the rhetorical brilliance of Shakespeare's language, but they're cine-literate and they can follow complex split narratives. The story needs to move faster than it used to. This production will be a cinematic version of the play; non-traditional and psychologically rooted, with little speaking out to the audience. Directors today have more tools. Without editing the text, tautologies can remain between what the actors are saying, and what the design is showing. So we can edit the text and find other ways to establish settings and describe the fantastical.

Two Versions of the Budget ➡

The fortnight before rehearsals begin, Natalie meets the creative team at Headlong's office in London.

Tom Scutt places the model box of his set design on the far end of a long conference table. The design resembles a Hollywood studio lot. The playing stage resembles a sound stage, within it a chair marked for the director, a camera on a dolly, a freestanding light, a scaffolding tower, a ladder and two large costume crates. A video screen can lower from the fly-tower to turn the stage, in effect, into a cinema.

As Tom puts the last miniatures on the set, the production manager, Felix Davies, arrives with the video designer, Ian William Galloway, and the lighting designer, David Holmes. Felix hands out two budgets, one that represents the ideal budget, and one that suggests a string of compromises. Even the cheaper version, which is twenty per cent cheaper than the other, is still substantially over-budget and so, for two hours, the team parses every join and every bolt of Tom's design, negotiating between the proposed set and the available budget.

The happy medium lies between big cuts that seem tempting at first but might create problems later – such as resisting the urge to save a few hundred pounds by buying a thinner floor that might not survive life on the road – and making tens of smaller cuts that seem insignificant at first but could, combined, 'unhinge' the whole aesthetic, such as cutting the number of costumes and wigs, or reducing the height of the scaffolding tower.

Having hired the team for its expert counsel, Natalie wants to hear what everyone has to say. Often, she remains silent for minutes at a time as she listens to the debate. 'I know only how to work collaboratively,' she says over lunch that day:

> Art isn't democratic in the sense that if you let everyone sway you, there can be no clarity, but the more ideas that come in, the better the show will be. I ask for all the ideas to be given and I choose what will best help realise my vision.

The First Day of Rehearsals ➡

'When you have your full company in rehearsals is when the journey and the work really begins,' Natalie says.

The litmus test was auditions. When Natalie met each potential company member, she explained her concept in as much depth as she could and stressed that the production would be no one's moment to 'give their Helena' (or whomever), but rather offer a chance to do Shakespeare as 'not everyone sees it'. Whilst rehearsal is 'a playground', the fundamentals of the production are non-negotiable. An actor who has not 'bought into' the production will struggle to generate ideas that are compatible with it or offer a performance that feels anything other than directed.

The company mixes actors with experience of traditional Shakespeare productions, and younger actors. At one end of the spectrum, there is Justin Avoth, who plays Theseus/Oberon, and observes the implied rhymes in the text ('nigh'/'immediately') and reads aloud with a resonant baritone voice. At the other end of the spectrum, there is Max Bennett, who plays Demetrius, and naturally speaks the text conversationally, breezily, as though it were contemporary speech.

The meet-and-greet is followed by a game. Sitting in a circle, the actors divide into pairs comprising an 'A' and a 'B' and share answers to a series of posed by Natalie, who also takes part. After each question, the As stay put whilst the Bs move clockwise to the freshly vacated chair and a new partner. Natalie's questions begin casually but soon, what began almost as speed-dating has become a discussion of the play and the production's aims. A few of the questions are:

- Did you get any good or bad Christmas presents this year? (Rehearsals began in early January.)
- Did you have any family arguments over Christmas?
- What do you dislike most about how Shakespeare is often presented in production?
- What was your first paid theatre job and what did you get paid?
- Do you believe in love at first sight; has it ever happened to you?
- Have you ever dated someone your family disapproved of?

- Can you remember a good or bad dream you've had?

With the play's themes percolating, the blinds are drawn and the company assembles around a television to watch excerpts from the documentary that accompanies the DVD release of the film *Cleopatra*. The footage introduces the extravagance to which *A Midsummer Night's Dream* will refer. We see Ancient Athens reconstructed over twenty acres at Pinewood Studios. We see hundreds of extras, costumed by garment workers who prepared Queen Elizabeth II for her coronation. We see the scale of intrusion into Richard Burton and Elizabeth Taylor's lives: the news reports, the paparazzi and shot after shot of the couple stepping out of cars to a crescendo of flashbulbs.

After lunch, the company sits around a large table to read the script aloud.

Work on the Script ➡

A typical day comprises two three-and-a-half-hour sessions divided by a one-hour lunch break.

The company begins by subdividing the scenes into events, which occur when a character enters or exits, or when something happens to change the balance of the relationships onstage, such as a new piece of information. Each event is given a title to encapsulate its tone and its principal action, such as *The Great Escape*, *Ugly as a Bear* and *The Kiss*.

The company agrees specific times and locations for each event, such as '7:30 p.m., Saturday, July 1962, main soundstage at the Athens Picture Company'. Everyone is encouraged to consider what time elapses between scenes and what their characters might be doing whilst they are offstage.

For much of the first week, the company translates each four-hundred-year-old line into modern English, beginning at the top:

> THESEUS. Now, fair Hippolyta, our nuptial hour
> Draws on apace; four happy days bring in
> Another moon – but O, methinks, how slow
> This old moon wanes! She lingers my desires,
> Like to a step-dame or a dowager
> Long with'ring out a young man's revenue.

The process does much of the work of traditional textual analysis by stealth. Reconfiguring the verse in language that is more readily understandable, and processing their initial reactions to both the characters and their situations, the company is laying foundations for performances that will be, for the most part, psychologically real.

However, this imperative occasionally creates problems, such as when the lovers awake from the dream, their enmity gone and their emotions suddenly rewired. Deirdre Mullins, who plays Helena, has difficulty making sense of her character's decision to accept Demetrius's love, given that he has given her little but insults. 'At the very least she'd be confused,' Deirdre reasons. 'She's been mocked too much to take anything at face value.' Natalie suggests a 'less full-on' gesture: 'Something that leaves space for a private reconciliation that comes later.' And so Deirdre plays her scepticism and Max Bennett (Demetrius) reconfigures what was an explanation as an apology to the girl he has offended. She touches his hand, but doesn't kiss him.

Sketches and Versions ➡

Natalie dislikes some of the established terminology of the director. She prefers *practice* to *rehearsal* and *suggestion* to *direction*. She cites the philosopher Socrates who, when put on trial for 'corrupting the nation's youth', argued that he never taught anyone anything, but was only midwife to their own thoughts and realisations. Actors inhabit roles, Natalie says, not directors; therefore the deepest and most rooted results come when an idea is shared. Her tools in rehearsal are questions:

- Do you think…?
- Should we…?
- Do we need to…?

The scenes are rehearsed in progressive drafts or 'sketches' as Natalie calls them, beginning with broad brushstrokes and adding more detail each time the company revisits a section. Natalie picks up on fractional shifts between sketches, and alters only one or two elements of the actors' performances to take the scene in another direction. A significant change in tone or in the characters' tactics marks a new *version* of that scene.

A week into rehearsals, Natalie is rehearsing Act 3, Scene 2, in which Puck (Sandy Grierson) tells Oberon (Justin Avoth) that he has bewitched the young Athenians with the love juice. Oberon gives him the antidote and sends him back into the field with a warning of dire consequences should he do anything but correct his mistake.

The stage directions place Oberon onstage at the beginning of the scene. Puck then enters. Are we to assume that Oberon summoned Puck and has waited for him at some appointed place, or that their meeting is by chance? Natalie, Sandy and Justin sketch each version, followed by a version that instead has Puck onstage first, lolling in Oberon's chair and Oberon entering in search of good news. This last option feels instinctively wrong as it inverts any master–servant relationship too early in the scene. Next, they sketch a version where Puck enters, terrified of punishment, aware he's done something wrong. This doesn't feel right either because it has no journey: it assumes that the characters know the content of the scene to come. They settle on a version where Puck bounds in, boasting of his fun at the human's expense. 'Expect Oberon to toast your success,' Natalie suggests to Sandy. But instead of toasting his success, Oberon accuses Puck of 'committing [his] knaveries wilfully.' The next sketch develops this idea, with Oberon grabbing Puck by the neck, and this in turn fuels a version that plays to Oberon's mercurial side: he sits in his chair and listens patiently as Puck 'pitches his latest feature'. Oberon applauds and, as Puck enjoys the adulation, the applause becomes a slow handclap. There is a pause. Then Oberon pounces.

Looking at the rehearsal from a distance, it it clear that much has been tried in the twenty minutes spent on it so far, and the ideas have evolved in steps:

1. *Puck sits in Oberon's chair*. Oberon arrives, nervous. Puck speaks and Oberon reacts immediately.

2. *Oberon sits in his chair*. Puck arrives, nervous. Oberon reacts immediately.

3. Oberon sits in his chair. Puck arrives, boastful. Oberon reacts immediately, *rebuking Puck*.

4. Oberon sits in his chair. Puck arrives, boastful. Oberon reacts immediately, *grabbing Puck by the collar*.

5. Oberon sits in his chair. Puck arrives, boastful. Oberon *waits, then pounces*, grabbing Puck by the collar.

The last version feels 'grounded,' Natalie says. 'Grounded and fresh.' She never tells an actor that an action is 'great', aware that the actor might cease to develop that part of performance, freezing it at the compliment. Instead, she compliments actors for being 'clear' or 'fresh' or 'exciting' or 'grounded', which allows the actor to keep searching for fresh insights.

The Lovers' Quarrel: Directing Chaos

A set piece of any production of *A Midsummer Night's Dream* is the lovers' four-way quarrel in Act 3, Scene 2. Demetrius and Lysander, under the influence of the love juice, compete for Helena's affection whilst Hermia tries to break through to Lysander who, only hours before, swore he loved Hermia.

The scene is physical comedy and the actors work up a sweat as they build on each other's ideas, experimenting with one zany idea after another. Lysander and Demetrius compete physically over Helena before they retreat to prepare for a duel with prop swords from the production of *Where the Wild Thyme Blows*. Hermia, for interfering, is locked in a costume crate and escapes, minutes later, wearing armour twice too large for her.

As the momentum takes the actors, the scene begins to feel muddy. Natalie, by contrast, is on the sideline, like a sports coach who can reach her players with words alone. The scene has to have integrity, she says. A trick reused too many times will soon feel 'dull as dishwater', and what feels fun and giddy in rehearsal may feel static onstage and bore the actors to repeat. 'It can't be just an amusing stage picture,' she says. Rather, the tactics should grow out of the character relationships. She leads a discussion of how Demetrius and Lysander one-up each other's declarations of love, which finds a physical expression in the two men fighting over who can declare their love from the highest, most 'romantic' point onstage, before degenerating into a cat-fight that is all the more ridiculous for taking place on a ladder.

Natalie gives the actors problems to solve. To help make the scene clearer, she asks what moments might be punctuated. What are the *points of no return*, where the stakes rise irreversibly? For example, once someone draws a sword, the characters can't go back to fighting with hands. Perhaps the last time someone called Hermia a 'puppet', she hospitalised them for it. Perhaps that's why Helena says it.

How to Make a Virtue of a Necessity ➡

A quirk of *A Midsummer Night's Dream* is that it ends with a subplot. Many productions of the play have been undone by the feeling that they peaked about thirty minutes before the end. The story proper ends in Act 4, Scene 1, after the dream ends and the lovers are reconciled. But there is still a scene in Act 4 plus a whole act to come. The dream ended, the film stars assemble on the sound stage, where production has wrapped on *Where the Wild Thyme Blows*. Under a huge banner that reads 'Just Married', Theseus, Hippolyta and the lovers watch the mechanicals perform *Pyramus and Thisbe*, the 'the most lamentable comedy, and most cruel death' of two lovers, separated by a wall, who meet under moonlight. After Thisbe is mortally wounded by a lion, Pyramus kills himself over her body.

The scene presents a huge logistical problem. In this production, the actors who play Lysander and Demetrius have so far doubled as the mechanicals, Snug and Snout. But all four characters, according to Shakespeare's script, attend the wedding. Before rehearsal, Natalie and Ben Power, then Headlong's associate director, prepared a version of the scene that aimed to solve both its dramaturgical and casting problems. In the subsequent draft, Quince becomes a quietly determined am-dram director and Bottom a frustrated sound recordist who mouthed along with the dialogue during filming and now imagines himself in its stars' gilt-edged costumes. Snug, Snout and Starveling are roped in to complete the cast, which gets progressively smaller: Starveling either forgets to turn up to the first rehearsal or changes his mind; Snug and Snout are scared away by the sight of Bottom transformed. By the end, only Bottom, Flute and Quince remain. Bottom plays Pyramus, Flute plays Thisbe and Quince plays everyone else: the narrator, the wall, the moon, and the lion. In this version, much of the tension and the charm come from watching Bottom step on other people's lines in his enthusiasm to give the Performance of His Life in front of his idols, whilst Quince juggles three roles and struggles to reign in his star.

Staying the Course →

The joy of rehearsals are the 'constant discoveries,' Natalie says:

> All preparation is theoretical. As a director, you come with your best proposal, which you want to throw out for something better as the actors think and find ways into the text to make it live and breathe. We've edited

> more of the text than I had the guts to do before we
> started and we've made discoveries about the
> performance style and the characters, and about what is
> scary and magical.

In the final days of rehearsal in London, the company runs the production twice in two days. These runs are for the actors more than for Natalie, to cement the work of rehearsal before the tech process 'pulls everything out of sync'.

Rupert Goold, Headlong's artistic director, attends the final run. His notes, Natalie says, are 'precise and incisive'; she agrees with 'ninety per cent' of them, which are mainly to do with clarifying who the mechanicals are and why they matter to the story. I ask her about the other ten per cent. She gives a diplomatic smile. 'The production isn't finished yet.'

With one week until the production opens at Southampton's Nuffield Theatre, the enormity of the task has hit home. The schedule has meant that rehearsal has been spent mostly staging scenes rather than working on text or on characters more generally. 'My brain feels like it's imploding trying to solve every moment,' Natalie says. 'I feel we've only scratched the surface.'

On the train to Southampton, Natalie emails the cast eighteen A4 pages of notes: an 'epic love letter' that works through the play scene by scene, addressing everything from broad, tonal concerns to minute details in individual performances. When the cast arrive at the venue a day later, they will find print-outs of the email waiting in their dressing rooms. Natalie does this to ensure that the actors have 'something to think about' during the short break before they travel to Southampton, and whilst they aren't needed for the tech; and to save time. The letter begins:

With a play like this, there is no downtime; we must start and end each scene with a bang. Lights and sound will finesse, but the impetus must come from the live action. Remember to pass the baton from section to section, scene to scene, to sustain the energy and momentum and, because we cut into the action at the most dynamic point of the scene, rev the energy to show there was already some preceding and crescendoing action.

Southampton ➡

The Nuffield Theatre sits at the heart of the campus of Southampton University. On the outside, it is a poster child for a utilitarian, brutalist 1960s design ethic. The fly-tower, all oxidised copper, juts into the sky from a square of raw concrete. Inside, the auditorium is wood-panelled, its ceiling an exposed latticework of pipes.

The creative team arrives twenty-four hours ahead of the actors. A friendly bed and breakfast a few miles from campus is home. Each morning, the team will assemble over breakfast to eat together and to talk of anything but theatre before deciding whether to walk up the hill to campus, or book a taxi. The taxi will usually win.

The Bastard Film ➡

The design team – Tom Scutt (set and costumes), Ian William Galloway (video), Tom Mills (sound) and David Holmes (lighting) – get into the theatre on the Sunday, keen to get as far ahead of the schedule as possible. Ian calibrates video projectors whilst David focuses lights and Tom Mills ricochets sound cues around the auditorium from speakers embedded in the walls.

Twice in the production, video sequences by Ian will take the strain of the storytelling. At the start of the performance, a cinema screen will lower from the fly-tower and Robin Goodfellow will nod to an unseen projectionist who starts the film.

Ian first got the callback when the concept involved a weather studio and green screens. A successful collaboration, he says, begins with a director who knows why they want to use video in a show, which is to say what its role will be, conceptually:

> Video design used to be expensive. Audiences wanted either to be tricked into believing that something was real, or be shown fantastic special effects. Now, the tools are ubiquitous. Anyone can shoot high-def video on their smartphone and edit it at home with free or cheap software. Because anyone can make something spectacular, spectacle is in itself no longer impressive. You can't get away with a design that's technically impressive in terms of graphics but suffers from a weak concept. Now, video can be declared, which is what we're doing with *A Midsummer Night's Dream*.

This first sequence comprises the opening credits of *Where the Wild Thyme Blows* and a scene from the film, each designed to mirror Mankiewicz's *Cleopatra*. Ian explains that the opening sequence 'telegraphs to the audience where we are and declares that, together, audience and company are going to conspire in creating a make-believe world, starting with the wry reproduction of a '50s film. Onscreen, Justin (Theseus-playing-sort-of-Richard-Burton-playing-sort-of-Mark-Antony) embraces Emily (Hippolyta-playing-sort-of-Elizabeth-Taylor-playing-sort-of-Cleopatra). They speak of love and then they kiss, and as the music swells behind them the lights onstage rise and the audience see the live actors onstage, only now we are on the soundstage at the Athens Picture Company, and the cameras are rolling on the day the footage was shot.

The draft edit of the footage is problematic. The first lines are Justin Avoth's. Theseus is addressing Hippolyta, but he is absent from the shot and so the audience cannot get its bearings, hearing only a disembodied voice as it looks at a close-up of Emily. Ian explains that when he shot the sequence, the intention was that the interaction between film and stage would be different. The film would be in conversation with the stage: it would almost 'grow out of the stage'. But between shooting and getting onstage, the opening sequence changed and Ian had to recut the video, stitching together a number of different takes to imply a flowing conversation. Now that the the concept has developed, the composite shots don't quite connect with one another. The footage was shot two weeks ago in the rehearsal studio. Although the sets and cameras are on site, there is no time to reshoot – the schedule is already managed down to the half-hour. Ian can only re-edit what he has and this is where he shows his ingenuity. Searching the alternate takes stored on his laptop, he works on a number of possible versions of the same scene.

A benefit of digital video technology is the speed with which a designer can experiment with and alter a video cue. Still, the process is stop-start. 'This bastard film,' Ian says as he prepares a new cut of the material and, for the fourth time, sets his laptop to render the footage in performance quality, which can take up to an hour. Ironically, although Natalie cannot see a proposal in full effect until long after she has asked for it, she can tell in seconds if the finished sequence isn't what she wants.

The final cut is shorter, and both interpolates alternate takes and crops some of the images differently. Having fixed the issue with the opening sequence, Ian moves on to designing a logo for the Athens Picture Company, and adjusting the 'beauty shots' of Helena and Hermia, which flicker hauntingly as thoughts of them bewitch Demetrius or Lysander.

Elsewhere, five whole video cues lay unused or cut on Ian's hard drive, including 'beauty shots' of each of the lovers and footage of Bottom, transformed by Puck's magic into an ass. Ian is unsentimental about the ideas altered or cut entirely. 'The question is always: does the clip work within the concept?' he says. 'Video has to be logical, so once you decide the concept, you have to maintain the through-line.' Initially, the logic of the video was to denote magic. The concept was developed to clarify magic in relation to the lovers, whose confusion is the motor of the story.

The God-mic ➡

One of the director's tools in tech rehearsal is the god-mic, which is a microphone routed to the entire auditorium, so-called because anyone on- or backstage could find themselves addressed by a booming, disembodied voice. Natalie resists using the god-mic for as long as possible. She distrusts it for its ability to obliterate in moments the close relationship that directors and actors build across a rehearsal process. Instead, she gives notes in dressing rooms, backstage, or at the lip of stage.

The god-mic has a pragmatic value, of course: it ensures that everyone hears the same instruction at the same time, and it preserves a director's voice. On the other hand, it introduces to a creative process the language of orders to be carried out.

Rehearsals in the rehearsal studio prioritise actors: they are conversations about characters and the indulgence of imagination through play. In production week, the ecosystem expands to include headphoned technicians, lighting plots and constructions in MDF. This comes at the worst possible time, Natalie says, when actors often want to go back to rehearsing so that they can acclimatise and adjust their performances to the space. The reality is that 'tech has to be the production team's rehearsal time,' Natalie says. 'Once you're in tech, it gets expensive.' I ask Natalie for the watchwords of a tech process and she answers, uncharacteristically, in short bursts: 'Pragmatic. Efficient. Every minute counts.' She watches the clock during tea breaks and reminds the company every time to return soon.

Some actors are patient; others are less willing to give up the power they had in the rehearsal room. They trudge and humph through every request, pointing at every half-finished prop as if the designer hasn't noticed, and framing complaints according to how any change may affect them specifically. Natalie 'feels her stomach knotting' on the second day as a few actors 'put their own anxieties above the piece'. She pushes harder than she usually would and devises with Rachael Presdee, the company stage manager, a tactic to separate rants from actual problems. To any complaint, they listen before asking calmly: 'And what do you think we should do about that?'

The plan is to work through one of the play's five acts in each three-hour tech 'session', but as the team finishes the second session with only half an hour of the production plotted, the plan begins to feel wildly ambitious. I ask whether anyone ever heard of a tech that completed on schedule. Chris Hill, the assistant director, says he once worked on a production that finished its tech process a day early. No one believes him. This is Arthurian legend, they say.

That evening, the production suffers a minor implosion. Natalie remains unerringly polite, but as she leaves the Nuffield, she is disheartened. She worries that the play cannot be done in as few tech sessions as the budget allows and that the technical ideas won't come together. That night, she struggles to sleep as she replays in her mind 'everything we did and everything we weren't able to do'. I only realise the extent of this weeks later when we reconstruct the evening. She speaks candidly, then asks that I omit her gravest doubts from the record. Then she thinks for a moment and tells me not to:

> This is what the job is. At this stage in a production process, my dreams are usually the scene changes on repeat, so to have had only one sleepless night is pretty good. But you *should* be sleepless about your shows. You have to be a perfectionist within your priorities. If you are sleeping comfortably, you probably don't care enough.

In a sense, the director is an actor too. 'The director has to have the most energy,' Natalie says the next morning. 'Even when she is shattered, the director has to keep everyone pushing forwards, *especially* if she can't get out of bed; *especially* when it's difficult.'

Clarity ➡️

Natalie attacks the next day with renewed energy. When the first session begins, she picks up the god-mic and returns the production to first principles: what would her mother, who doesn't know the play, understand and struggle to understand? 'You interrogate every decision, and if something isn't sorted, you do it again,' she says. 'What event in the production could be clearer?'

The answer for her is Bottom's transformation. The scene begins with the mechanicals rehearsing *Pyramus and Thisbe*. Bottom, who is in this production a sound recordist on *Where the Wild Thyme Blows*, steps into a sound-recording booth where he is transformed by Puck. He emerges in monstrous form, an ass's head in place of his own. The rest of the group run in fear and Bottom is left alone. He sings to raise his spirits and his song wakes Titania, who falls immediately in love with him, poisoned by the love juice. Bottom's song in this production is 'Up on the Roof', a buoyant pop song about finding a sanctuary away from the pressures of society, made famous in 1962 by The Drifters.

The logic of Bottom's transformation is unclear, Natalie reasons. The first part of the solution is relatively simple and comes from Sandy Grierson, who plays Puck, and who has responded instantly to the increase in pace. Puck is to become more active in the scene. Before, he lingered in the shadows; now he moves downstage which alone helps refocus him as the agent of Bottom's transformation. Puck addresses the audience directly and stops time with clicks of his fingers. To transform Bottom, he takes a fur stole from around Flute's neck, and a screwdriver from Snout's toolbox, and follows Puck into the crate, from which we hear the sounds of welding and banging. In rehearsal, this process of joining the dots feels almost remedial, but when the special effects, costumes and physical action arrive, it can be important to revisit the narrative to ensure that its action is sufficiently streamlined.

With this challenge solved, Natalie turns to a technical problem with the scene. Tom Mills (composer/sound designer) has recorded an instrumental track for Chris (Bottom) to sing over, but where the music comes from within the logic of the production has never been quite clear. In addition, the volume of the track overpowers Chris's voice, no matter how well he projects.

Natalie unlocks the trickster in Puck to solve both puzzles. 'The music should come from Puck,' she says, and indeed, for him to simply remain onstage whilst Chris sings seems to unlock the possibility of magic. What seemed strange yesterday, when Chris started to sing with a full unseen backing band, now seems logical. Puck fetches a boom mic used in the scenes in the film studio, and follows Bottom as he sings. The prop microphone contains a working microphone, and so Chris's voice is sufficiently amplified to combine with the recorded track.

A Midsummer Night's Dream in Performance ➡

Natalie hopes for as large an audience as possible at the first preview performance. 'The more people there are, the more I'll know about the show.' As the lights in the auditorium fade, I notice a memorial inscribed on the seat in front: to a loving husband and father; a man 'who loved a show'. A few hours ago, the auditorium was filled with cardboard coffee cups and makeshift desks. Now there is a sizable audience flicking through their programmes and looking expectantly at a red-velvet curtain – the good people who want 'a show'.

Excepting a misfiring sound cue and some flabby transitions between scenes, the first performance goes smoothly. The company unwinds in the students' union (it's karaoke night) before heading to bed in progressive waves of taxis. They are called at two p.m. tomorrow to work through Natalie's notes from the first preview.

The story of *A Midsummer Night's Dream* in preview is a journey of small adjustments underpinned by a few structural changes. Now that the play feels psychologically real, Natalie works to fine-tune the comedy and sense of visceral performance.

Sound

A well-chosen piece of music can create momentum between scenes or prepare the audience for tonal changes between scenes. The mechanicals' arrival in the wood has so far been accompanied by a sombre melody, played on the French horn. But what follows is comedy. After a few performances, in which the mechanicals' scene seems to fall flat despite the actors' best efforts, Tom Mills, the composer, repurposes a cue from elsewhere in the score, a lighter and more up-tempo piece of music that cleanses the palate of the last scene, which was emotional drama, and prepares the audience for the next course, which is comedy. The change is enormous.

Conversely, a feature of the sound design is cut, in which the physical closeness of fairies and mortals produces an intense electrical hum, as if two magnetic fields – two worlds – are interfering with one another and pushing each other back to where they belong. However, in performance it becomes evident that the moment when a mortal and a fairy are close is when Oberon takes pity on Helena. It is a moment of sympathy. Although an elegant design solution, here the hum is deemed 'oppressive' and so it is cut.

Pyramus and Thisbe

After four performances, Natalie decides to strengthen the connection between *Pyramus and Thisbe* and *Where the Wild Thyme Blows*. One element of this is replacing the live music that David Shaw Parker's Quince plays on guitar during the performance with a reel-to-reel audio player loaded with sound effects and orchestral cues from *Where the Wild Thyme Blows*. David takes the news gracefully: he asks only that the guitar stay on tour for him to play backstage.

As a group, the actors in *Pyramus and Thisbe* are hostile to the suggestion of introducing recorded, filmic underscoring. The production is, on the whole, high-concept and technologically complex. *Pyramus and Thisbe* is enjoyably low-tech and they defend the scene as they rehearsed it for that simplicity. Music, they say, would make the scene 'too professional' and they are hesitant to try anything new in performance that evening; a few people are hesitant even to try it once in rehearsal.

Natalie listens to each complaint and then she smiles as she speaks. Unruffled. Unrufflable. I wonder if she would let the cast know if she had even a headache.

Sometimes, a director feels 'a bit like a card player,' she will say that evening as the audience enters.

> When directing I often feel like I'm playing cards – there are fifty-two cards in the pack and fifty-odd ways to play. The fifty-second card reads 'This is the way I want this done', but I've never played that card and it's important to me that I don't. I'd rather question and guide.

The audience must be the arbitrator, she says. She pushes and for an hour the group rehearses a version of *Pyramus and Thisbe* with filmic underscoring. That evening, Pyramus and Thisbe kiss to a swell of music that recalls Theseus and Hippolyta in *Where the Wild Thyme Blows* and the sequence wins its first round of applause.

Forging Forwards ➡

A Midsummer Night's Dream opens at the Nuffield Theatre after six preview performances. After press night, the creative team hands over to the actors, the stage-management team and Chris Hill, who will see the production into each tour stop. Natalie revisits the tour every other week.

We meet two months later, as the production arrives in Cambridge for its final week of performances. Natalie reflects on the enormity of the project: not only was *A Midsummer Night's Dream* her first production of a Shakespeare play, it was also her first touring production and it employed the largest company of actors she has ever worked with, telling a story in five acts, across two-and-a-half hours – which is significantly longer than the 'one-act, ninety-minute prose pieces' to which she is accustomed. The learning curve, she says, was exponential in terms of working with a concept, and learning what can be achieved with limited time.

The production was full of strong choices, aesthetically and editorially. Natalie said as rehearsals began that not everyone would like this production. Not everyone did. The press response was mixed, with the reviews ranging from two stars in the *Guardian* up to five on whatsonstage.com.

For many directors, the experience of opening a newspaper or a webpage to read a review remains as visceral as the first time it happens. 'The first show I ever directed got bad reviews,' Natalie says. 'I remember I wanted to hide in my bedroom and pull my duvet over my head.' However, the experience taught her that a director cannot derive her adrenaline rush from a good review. 'Critics change,' she says. 'Artistic directors change. You are the only person going through your own life, and so you have to make work that you're proud of. You have to be your own barometer and your own harshest critic.'

Whilst the production was, for the most part, technically elaborate, Natalie is most pleased with the scenes that seem most earthbound: the mechanicals' performance of *Pyramus and Thisbe*, the lovers' quarrel, the psychological quality of many interactions between characters.

If she could direct the production again, she might have allowed the film references and homages to develop across the production instead of being front-loaded in the opening scene. Natalie reflects that a director and designer may devise a concept which seems so clear in their heads, but which may not necessarily be so clear to the audience. She might have clarified that Lysander is Demetrius's stunt double. Instead of 'Just Married', the festooning at the mechanicals' performance might have read 'It's a Wrap!', 'because Shakespeare tells us it's a wedding and "It's a Wrap" would have underscored the film idea.'

But a director cannot do it again. She can only learn and progress to the next project.

I fear I'm botching the interview. Today should be a celebration of the production, and I have introduced the language of the post mortem. Natalie smiles the unruffable smile I know from the tech process.

> I try to take as much from the experience as I can for the next time I direct a production. There are always things you could have understood better or directed better, some of which you know as you go into rehearsal, some you realise as you're watching, and some you don't comprehend until after the event. There were places we could've gone further and places where we should have pulled back. A production has so many elements, and skills are so personal that everyone will

find a different approach. You can't know what the right approach would have been until you've had the experience. You just have to do it and learn. You might see my show or anyone's show and see all the pitfalls and know how to avoid them, then fall into a pitfall of your own in the future. I've not enjoyed rehearsals so much in a long time and I'm proud of the production. A director is forever on a journey, and you're the only person on that journey, so you need to keep forging forwards.

Nikolai Foster

Great Expectations

by Tanika Gupta
after Charles Dickens

English Touring Theatre and
Watford Palace Theatre on tour

Nikolai Foster was born in Copenhagen and grew up in North Yorkshire. He trained at Drama Centre London and at the Crucible, Sheffield.

He has been director on attachment at the Crucible, the Royal Court Theatre and the National Theatre Studio, and is an associate director of the West Yorkshire Playhouse, Leeds.

Nikolai has directed *Merrily We Roll Along* (Clwyd Theatr Cymru), *The Diary of Anne Frank* (York Theatre Royal and the Touring Consortium), *All the Fun of the Fair* (on tour), *Flashdance* (West End), *A Christmas Carol* (Birmingham Rep), *Kes* (Liverpool Playhouse and on tour), *Amadeus* and *Assassins* (Crucible), *Aspects of Love* (UK tour and Nelson Mandela Theatre, Johannesburg), and *Annie, Animal Farm, Salonika* and *Bollywood Jane* (West Yorkshire Playhouse).

'The director's job is to serve a play with imagination, intelligence and integrity, and challenge a text, his actors and collaborators, to create original work that is relevant to the world we live in.'

Nikolai Foster

Simone James (Estella) and Lynn Farleigh (Miss
Havisham)

Great Expectations
by Tanika Gupta after Charles Dickens

Opened at Watford Palace Theatre on 17 February 2011.

Creative
Director **Nikolai Foster**
Designer **Colin Richmond**
Lighting Designer **Lee Curran**
Composer **Nicki Wells**
Musical Advisor **Nitin Sawhney**
Sound Designer **Sebastian Frost**
Casting Director **Kay Magson**
Movement and Choreography **Zoobin Surty** and **Cressida Carré**
Fight Director **Kate Waters**
Associate Director **Nicola Samer**

Cast
Magwitch **Jude Akuwudike**
Compeyson **Rob Compton**
Herbert Pocket **Giles Cooper**
Jaggers **Russell Dixon**
Miss Havisham **Lynn Farleigh**
Mrs Gargery/Molly **Pooja Ghai**
Estella **Simone James**
Joe Gargery **Tony Jayawardena**
Pip **Tariq Jordan**
Pumblechook **Shiv Grewal**
Wemick **Darren Kuppan**
Biddy **Kiran Landa**

A Director in Commercial Theatre ➜

When I meet Nikolai Foster in a tea shop in Soho, he is two hours off the train from the opening of his production of *A Christmas Carol* at the West Yorkshire Playhouse. He has an hour before he is due at the nearby Shaftesbury Theatre where his production of *Flashdance* opened a few months before, and before he goes home he will cram in a quick meeting for the production of *Macbeth*, which he is to direct in Singapore immediately after *Great Expectations*.

When Nikolai joins the production, the wheels are already in motion, and turning fast. The creative process is new, but the machine moves fast and has to be fed. Ideally, a director would have time to read and re-read a play and immerse himself in its world, but often the reality is that the director in touring theatre must acclimatise material fast to the familiar schedule: four weeks of rehearsal, three days of tech and the imperative that the set must fit in a lorry and be able to be constructed in three hours. Fortunately, with his experience in commercial theatre, where hiring the director can be the last piece of a puzzle that begins with producers, Nikolai is familiar with that often brutal framework, and with the process of creating space for an artistic process within it.

A Story of India ➡

This play is *Great Expectations*, adapted from Charles Dickens' novel by Tanika Gupta.

The production's 'big idea' is to relocate the action from Victorian England to colonial India. Nikolai reflects that the scale of that decision affects his role on the project:

> I don't need to manufacture a 'take' on the material. The adaption is bold; so different from the Dickens we know. The location is so evocative. As a theatregoer, I would like to be transported to 1800s Calcutta. The idea of Miss Havisham as a colonial ex-pat meeting a young Indian boy is theatrically exciting… If I'm the student writing the school essay, I've got enough to consider – I don't need the director making another statement on top of it. I would hate for that to sound lazy, but there is only so much concept a play can take. *The play is the thing*, and part of the director's job is knowing how much or little of his hand a play can cope with. My job on this production is to keep the story moving and ensure that the scenes are truthful, detailed and exciting.

This is no small task. The script is heavy enough that it produces a thud when it lands on a table. It is a 'beast': a thirty-three-scene epic following twelve years of a life lived against the backdrop of a country moving towards the end of colonial rule. It is also a love story, a coming-of-age story, a story of political struggle and a treatise on class.

The Storyboard ➡

The production begins proper with a storyboard. This document, conceived alone by Nikolai, is a kind of scale model that posits the tone of the production and imagines the transition between scenes. On a prosaic level, that means how the production will get from scene to scene. More artistically, it means finding the tone of the production. If there are any moments in the script that don't feel theatrical, Nikolai wants to find them first on the page.

Extract from the storyboard

Act 1, Scene 1

Setting: India, 1861

Entering the theatre, the audience is confronted with what appears to be a traditional front cloth. On closer inspection, this is a large series of individual pieces of material, stitched together by hand, to make a huge collage of colour and zigzag landscapes, which could be a map of the World.

A delicate shaft of light zips across the cloth, gently warming it and pulling out the hotchpotch of stitching. We can see nothing beyond. Nor can we hear anything.

Gently, the house lights start to fall away. Music is heard in the distance – perhaps a lone guitar? A fusion of electronic sounds? Whatever it is, it should be solitary, distant and thoughtful. Music fills the room and a lone female voice is heard singing on top of the music. It drifts through the warm air.

A single light/spot comes up behind the front cloth. A young boy, Pip, sits on his haunches. He stares into the distance, alone with his thoughts. He is almost frozen in time and space.We hold this image of the child and the warm light soaring above him as the music continues.

In the distance, a figure approaches. His hands and feet are shackled. There is a huge light-source directly behind the figure, which causes a terrific shadow to hit the back of the front cloth.

Two images: The boy on the ground with the light towering above him and the more abstract silhouette of a giant on the front cloth.

The music continues as the images hold our focus, only the voice fades away.

As the actors speak, the music becomes underscore and is much more menacing and fragmented.

Magwitch speaks and on his second line we start to open out the space to a much more naturalistic state.

As the lights illuminate the graveyard, we see skulls scattered about the floor. A pyre smokes gentle, upstage-left. (NB. The pyre needs to be practical so an actor can sit/stand on it.) It is difficult to make out what these objects are in the dim, hazy, silvery moonlight. There should be no sense of where the boundaries of this space are.

The scene should feel dreamlike and surreal. We are experiencing the scene through a child's imaginative and distorted eyes. The underscore/sounds should continue throughout.

As Magwitch exits, the underscore starts to build and suddenly leaps into something dynamic and fast-moving (percussive?). It carries us through the fearful night, Pip's nightmares, and into the calm of the next day.

Pip runs offstage.

Simultaneously, the scene shifts. Pip crosses the stage, pulling the front cloth with him as he goes, revealing the new scene and with this, the lights come up. (NB. This change must last no more than forty-five seconds.)

For Nikolai, a production is clearest when its tone and aesthetic comes from one mind. 'The few times I've worked with someone who didn't share the concept, it's been the elephant in the room,' he says, and so he builds a team that might 'better' his vision within the boundaries he has set. As soon as rehearsals begin, the storyboard is put away in search of something better.

The design, by Colin Richmond, is a poetic rendering of an Indian village ('simple and uncluttered') that will use light and music to bind its sparse environment together and drive the transitions between scenes. Seven doors, in colonial style, are suspended upstage and can be lowered to become functional. Three silk curtains on rails can be brought in to work with the lighting to define smaller spaces and imply, for example, the corridors of Miss Havisham's crumbling mansion. The result is a production that will move at filmic speed, revealing locations as the curtain wipes across the stage.

Rehearsals ➡

The rehearsal room at English Touring Theatre's building in South London is full with representatives from each of the tour venues: one more person and the atmosphere would tip into uncomfortable. Brigid Larmour, the artistic director of Watford Palace Theatre, invites the audience to enjoy 'the particular magic' of hearing a new play spoken for the first time.

Nikolai invites the actors to disregard any received notions they might have about Dickens' characters. Adamant that this version should be treated as a new play, rather than as a 'Hallmark version of the novel', he asks the company to consider today a 'celebration of ambition': the ambition of Dickens' vision, the ambition of Tanika's adaptation and the producers' ambition in assembling an uncommonly large cast (twelve) for a touring production.

Then Nikolai does something I've not seen before. Instead of trying to hide his fear of the first day of rehearsals behind humour, bravado or shuffling indifference, he does the opposite: he expresses to the room the terror he feels, describing the sleepless night he has had and the cold sweat he has felt since four a.m. Instead of sharing worried looks, the actors appear to relax a notch. A younger member of the company breathes out as if released from a vice.

I ask Nikolai about this when we break for lunch. Is this a strategy? 'Yes,' he says, although it is also true:

> I'm frightened every time. Directing a play is a big responsibility. You start with words on a page and in six weeks you have to have this fully fledged entity that none of us can see today. Every first day I think: 'Why do I do this job?' The first few times I had to stand up in front of a room of actors, I felt I'd burst. Now it's a way of breaking the ice and naming that fear so it can become something useful. Besides, I like being frightened... There's something masochistic about that, isn't there?

Readthrough ➡️

The *Great Expectations* rehearsal room operates one golden rule: the cast must be brave and willing to 'throw themselves over the edge'. Getting egg on their faces is part of the fun.

The first three days are spent reading and discussing the script. 'Don't be afraid of asking dumb questions,' Nikolai says. 'I'll be asking loads myself.'

The decision to relocate the action to India moves the story out from under Dickens' shadow, creating exciting possibilities for the actors to create new and distinct characters. However, given the colonial setting, the temptation is to cast the British characters in the uncomplicated role of the oppressor. Nikolai advocates caution when the discussion arises, asking the actors to be careful that they present 'not only what is bad about these characters, but also what is good about them'. He cites the example of Jaggers, the British lawyer dropped, ill-prepared, into Indian life. Jaggers could be interpreted as a manifestation of British imperialism – a pantomime villain – but not only would that be boring, it would ignore the good that Jaggers tries to spread through his actions. Similarly, the notion of removing Pip from his village at the behest of a wealthy benefactor might well fit our modern understanding of human trafficking but, in Dickens' time, when the alternative is the workhouse, it might be the least worst option. 'Every character has a story,' Nikolai says. 'Every character is vulnerable. That's why the story is interesting. There are always two sides and they are equally charged.'

Work on Scenes ➡

Having become aware of the play intellectually through the reading process, the task of rehearsal turns to expanding the text in physical space. Nikolai prepares to rehearse a scene by reading the script ahead of time, paying attention to two questions:

- What *happens* in the scene? – What are the plot events vital to telling the story? What takes the story from A to B?
- What is this scene *about*? – This could be, for example, something in the political undercurrent of the scene, or a theme in the writing, or a moment in a character's emotional journey.

Scene 1 finds Pip, aged twelve, playing in the deserted grounds of a crematorium near his village. A voice booms from the dark and, before Pip can run, Magwitch emerges from the river. He threatens Pip into stealing him food and a file.

Often, Nikolai will begin by pitching a version of the scene that he would like to see the actors explore. That might include an indication of tone, even some elements of blocking. He directs Tariq Jordan, who plays Pip:

> Explore what it is to play. Discover the skull on the
> ground in front of you. Imagine that this is the first time
> you've seen a human skull this close. It reminds you of
> your mum and dad and therefore the playground
> suddenly becomes a sinister place; then you stop and
> you cry.

As the rehearsal unfolds, Nikolai barely touches his script. Before a production goes into rehearsal, and before exploring each scene, he reads the script enough that he doesn't need to refer to it. Earlier in his career, Nikolai would follow the words on the page as the actors spoke, holding on to the script 'as if it was going to tell me what I should do'. Then, a few years ago, he decided to put away what had become a security blanket. 'I want to be intuitive and open to what's going on,' he says. 'That means observing and working in the moment. I don't think I even glance at the script any more.' Once he did so, he says, he relaxed and began to notice and respond more to the mood of the room.

Part of Nikolai's professional journey has been to trust his instincts, which are a director's 'best tool' in the rehearsal room. 'Theatre should be original and truthful and theatrical and beautiful and relevant,' he says. 'Those are the principles. Beyond that, there is only intuition.'

What is the scene *about*?

Scene 10 visits Pip and his childhood friend Biddy as teenagers. They are sitting on the riverbank near the village. Pip is reading a book in English; Biddy is writing her diary. By this point in the story, Pip is visiting Miss Havisham regularly, and has started to embrace British culture. Biddy accuses Pip of neglecting his Indian heritage and when Pip defends British culture, she challenges him to teach her an English dance.

On the surface, the scene is about three things: cultural assimilation, updating a friend on what's happened since they last saw each other, and sharing the relative oddity of European dancing. The script tells you that much. However, the scene only comes alive when the company goes deeper into the material and explores unrequited love: for Biddy, each hour Pip spends with Miss Havisham takes him further from the village and from her. Paradoxically, the more Pip includes Biddy in what he has learned, the more distant she feels from him.

Nikolai works with Tariq (Pip) and Kiran Landa (Biddy) to find a physical expression of that growing divide, and of Biddy's affection. They try a version of the scene in which Biddy cannot look Pip in the eyes as they dance, then a version in which she can *only* look him in the eye. Nikolai directs by asking Kiran to focus her attention on how Tariq's hand feels in hers. The charge of the scene begins to shift. Lines sharpen in their importance and the relationship is threaded into the audience's mind, and so, a few minutes later, when Pip describes Estella, Miss Havisham's adopted daughter, as 'the most beautiful girl in the world', we are primed not to look at Pip but at Biddy for her response.

Another example of unlocking a scene is Act 2, Scene 4, in which Joe Gargery visits Pip in Calcutta to bring news of Mrs Gargery's death. Pip's roommate, Herbert Pocket, lets Joe into the flat and the two share an awkward moment as they wait for Pip. Herbert offers a handshake but Joe bows. An Englishman, Herbert offers Joe a drink ('tea or coffee?') and Joe is too polite to 'inconvenience' Herbert by expressing a preference either way. So far, so sitcom. Again, the scene comes alive with a subtle shift of emphasis that comes from diving deeper into Tanika's script: Giles Cooper (Herbert) suggests that Herbert has become so comfortable in Calcutta that he forgets that Joe may be a stranger to the cosmopolitan. Nikolai directs this by having Herbert treat Joe immediately as though he were an old friend. Joe responds uneasily, hovering at the door as he waits for Pip. When they next rehearse the scene, Joe's small-town subservience to a colonial 'master' disappears. Instead, Tony Jayawardena (Joe) plays the propriety and dignity of a man who is uncomfortable in the company of a member of another caste.

Rehearsing in layers

A lot happens in Act 1, Scene 4. The villagers are dancing in seasonal celebration of the goddess Kali when Magwitch and Compeyson crash on to the stage, locked in a fight to the death. The crowd scatters. Compeyson, hampered by his leg irons, looks to be a dead man until two army officers run on and separate the prisoners seconds before Magwitch can deliver the killing blow. The sequence involves eleven of the company's twelve actors, live fire effects, dance and a brutal fight sequence.

It takes a day to assemble the scene, which is created in layers that are combined late in the afternoon. In one room, Zoobin Surty, the choreographer, rehearses the villagers' dance whilst, in another room, the fight director, Kate Waters, rehearses Jude (Magwitch) and Rob (Compeyson), who wears rough-and-ready leg irons made from fabric and string.

When Rob and Jude are safely in control of the choreography, they add the text and, when they can fight and speak the text at the same time, Zubin and Nikolai start to slot the villagers around them. Only when the stage is physically safe for everyone does Nikolai discuss ad-libs from the crowd.

To avoid generic crowd acting, Nikolai assigns each actor a *task*, which is a playable action that has an end. Instead of asking the actors to 'act scared of Magwitch', for example, he will ask them to 'keep as far from Magwitch as possible'. To add definition to the guards' performance, he discusses the detail that the pair are outnumbered by villagers and that their rifles hold only one shot each. If they shoot and miss, they could be overpowered. When the scene plays again, there are nervous glances and twitchy trigger fingers. Even if the audience does not notice the exact detail, these moments sculpt the scene and lend it definition.

Threading a relationship

The first time the company rehearses the end of the play, in which Pip and Estella meet on the streets of Calcutta years after the main action of the play, it registers as a 'damp squib'. Nikolai works backwards through the play, looking at each scene that places Pip and Estella onstage together or references their relationship. He resolves to reinvestigate those moments and create clearer lines in their relationship.

Scene 11 finds Pip, now sixteen years old, standing with Joe Gargery before Miss Havisham and Estella in Miss Havisham's mansion. Miss Havisham pays Pip for his services and informs him that he will no longer be called upon to visit. Pip steals a look at Estella who appears withdrawn but does not meet his eye. Simone James, who plays Estella, suggests that Miss Havisham is testing Estella's loyalty by making her watch as she exiles Pip. She finds this justification in Miss Havisham's question to Estella:

> MISS HAVISHAM. What do you think of young Pip?
>
> ESTELLA. I hate him.

> MISS HAVISHAM. Break their hearts, my pride and hope.
> Break their hearts and have no mercy!

Nikolai asks to see a version of the scene in which they physicalise their emotions overtly. The exercise, not intended for performance, allows the actors to share their thought processes and allow the resulting discoveries to be threaded back into the scene. Simone emphasises the difficulty of the choice that she is being forced to make by taking much longer to reply to Miss Havisham's questions. Her performance suggests that she knows that Miss Havisham is testing her, and almost that her body itself is battling to stop her mouth forming the words that are her surrender. She finds a physical release when Miss Havisham asks to be handed her purse and Simone slams the bag into Lynn Farleigh's (Miss Havisham's) hand. Lynn is taken aback by the strength of Simone's rebellion. She makes a discovery: Estella is not so malleable as Miss Havisham thought. She suggests:

> Perhaps Pip's presence is a threat to her life with Estella. Maybe Miss Havisham has clocked Estella's raging hormones and decided that Pip has to go?

This awareness, shared by Simone and Lynn, changes Estella's role in the scene irreversibly.

Watching rehearsals one day, Tanika suggests that Pip's kiss with Estella in Act 2 should change from a peck on the check into a full-blown, swept-off-the-feet moment, and together they redraw a scene in Act 2, in which Pip confronts Miss Havisham about her effect on Estella over the years, for not equipping her with the empathy for love; for removing the language of vulnerability and trust from her vocabulary altogether. Before, Pip spoke to Miss Havisham. Now, Pip addresses Estella directly, even as he vents at Miss Havisham. The effect is that the audience sees Pip put his heart on the line and 'lose' Estella once again.

The combined effect is that, when we see them in the final scene, there is a stronger sense that we are seeing them as lovers to be reunited, rather than united for the first time. Nikolai coaches: 'This is Estella's last chance to say what she wants to say to Pip', and, as an exercise, he asks Tariq to turn away from Simone, and to resist turning back until Simone can win him round using only the text and her voice.

Reordering Dialogue ➡

The process of rehearsal has been to take a play that is, on the page, intellectually 'heavy', and find a staging that is 'light and sparky'. In the first weeks, stage directions and even dialogue are progressively scaled back as the actors take on the job of telling the story using all their bodies, and whole sections of the dialogue – themes, confessions, longings – become implicit. Nikolai explains that an actor can 'embody a moment briefly in the action, and everyone sees it, and "gets" it, and it's done'.

'The play is the thing,' Nikolai says, and writers deserve 'profound respect' because 'they're the people who sit in the room with the blank paper'. However, directing the West End musical *Flashdance* in 2009, Nikolai's attitude towards collaboration developed:

> With *Flashdance* we were putting new changes in on press night and that gave me confidence. The writer thinks about how the play is going to work, but as the director I'm thinking in a different way whilst serving the writing. As long as your motivation is to serve the playwright, I think you can roll up your sleeves and get a bit mucky.

Tanika is not always present when Nikolai suggests a cut or a small change to the script, although he keeps her up to date through emails and rehearsal notes. When Tanika visits rehearsals one day I ask her whether she minds directors making small cuts to the script. She laughs. 'Oh, please, they're hardly big speeches!'

That day, Tanika has cuts of her own. She snips at a few scenes and cuts a few of Magwitch's longer speeches ('his theatrical arias,' she says), where he diverges from the topic at hand, or moves the conversation into back-story. 'Too many of those moments and he reads as a man who likes the sound of his own voice.' Later that week, no one notices when Jude accidentally skips half a page of text in which Magwitch describes the fear of living as a fugitive. When Jude confesses, Nikolai springs up and fetches his script. Jude recites the same passage, skipping the same passage on purpose and Nikolai agrees that the thoughts still connect. Tanika shouts from the other side of the room, 'I didn't miss it!' – and a mistake becomes a good edit.

Directness ➡️

Directors differ in how much they include actors in the wider ecosystem of production. How much, for example, does it help the company to know about what the designer is up to? Directors, who are responsible for the production as a whole, often move between rehearsals and production meetings without allowing a concern in one area to carry into another.

Nikolai is perhaps more open about production pressures than most, and he mollycoddles no one. One Monday morning in the second week of rehearsals, concentration disintegrates. The cast are rehearsing a complex fight sequence and a general lack of focus spreads across the room, not only wasting time but increasing the chance of Jude and Rob, the fighters, getting hurt. Nikolai asks the company, 'out of respect for me, for each other and for the show to shut up'. He says that last part clearly and slowly, leaving no room for the possibility that he's joking. Immediately there is silence. He continues: 'There are production pressures outside this room – I shield you from those – but there is pressure on me and on this production, so I don't mind if you talk but do it outside.'

A few weeks later, I bring up the episode. 'Theatremakers create fragile, beautiful things,' he says, 'but that doesn't mean it's not a business':

> It takes skill to construct a play or realise a production. I worry that something is being missed in how some younger actors are being trained because they think that everything in a production has to be 'about them' or about 'how they feel', and that should never be the case. Everything we do must be to serve the play. Most older actors get a scene working practically, then get on with it. And with some – the tough old birds – it's like preparing for battle. You'll see them climbing into their costumes, slapping on the make-up and smoking a cigarette before they go on for the next scene, whilst the stagehands are hoiking sets on wires and making them disappear into the fly-tower. I love that juxtaposition between what you see onstage and what you see backstage. If something isn't working, you find a way to mend it.

After Nikolai reprimands the cast, the atmosphere changes, but no one sulks. The rehearsal picks up where it left off with renewed focus.

When I tell people I am observing Nikolai at work, the comment I hear most is that 'actors love him'. I wonder if that directness is part of the reason. He never talks down to anyone and this sensibility carries into the type of notes he gives. Rehearsing the scene, late in the play, in which Pip visits Magwitch in prison, Tariq presents a version of Pip that reverts to a scared boy. His performance is detailed and believable, but perhaps not what the scene needs. Nikolai steps in. 'Lighten up a bit!' he says and laughs openly. 'You don't need to remind Magwitch that he's going to be hanged next week – he knows!' Tariq starts laughing too. Another director might choose to communicate such a note through a series of questions – to disguise worry, to convince Magwitch through nonchalance that he will not be hanged – but Nikolai opts for one sentence delivered half as a joke. Similarly, when he wants Jude to help communicate to the audience that months have passed since we last saw Magwitch, and that Magwitch is gravely ill, he says only: 'You need to degenerate more.' Jude nods: 'Okay, I can do that.' And he does it.

Watford Palace Theatre ➡️

After two weeks in the rehearsal studio at English Touring Theatre's headquarters in London, the company relocates to Watford Palace where *Great Expectations* will open in three weeks. Nikolai feels ambivalent: on one hand, he is overjoyed that the play, which felt 'heavy' on the page, feels 'light' onstage, 'almost like a different play'. On the other hand, *it feels like a different play*. 'It's not the production I'd imagined,' he says, and he is destabilised by the realisation. 'Now I know how the play reads onstage, I can see that it needs a lot more life and bounce in the music and particularly in the movement between scenes.'

At this stage, the production's sound designer Sebastian Frost joins rehearsal each day. The music is composed by Nicki Wells, a young British composer who lived in India for a time as a child and brings to the project a working knowledge of the culture and the language that manifests in melodic and percussive snatches of music that, like Pip's mind, are a conversation between India and the West. Sebastian's job in rehearsal is to integrate the music into the production and expand the composer's work to fill the space, manipulating different elements of the physical sound so that it can rumble and roll around the auditorium.

Sebastian watches the cast drill a difficult scene transition. It is the opening of Act 2 and we are on the streets of Calcutta. Pip has arrived from his village and is met by Wemick, who is clerk to the lawyer, Jaggers, Pip's protector in the city. Wemick calls for Pip to accompany him to Jaggers' office and suddenly music rushes in. The cast sweep across the stage and in five seconds, the bustling streets of Calcutta become Jaggers' office. Nikolai announces each lighting change as Sebastian times the speed of the transition. As Nikolai tweaks the transition, Sebastian alters the cue. Adept with music-editing software, Sebastian can offer solutions in minutes.

A few hours later, Nikolai decides that another piece of transition music should be altered. The scene is Pip and Estella meeting in Calcutta, and the music that ends their interaction is a motif that represents them as a couple. The next scene is Magwitch arriving to shatter Pip's new life in Calcutta. 'The earth is about to open,' Nikolai says. 'The music cue needs to prefigure that.' With the entire score stored on hard drive, Sebastian and Nicki cycle through the cues to find another piece of music entirely, one that could drive the transition more forcefully. The two cues are combined. Estella and Pip leave the stage to a spirited, societal Viennese Waltz that twists and distorts into percussion and the sound of wind battering the walls of Pip's flat and rain drumming on the windows.

Week Five ➡️

On the first day of the final week in the rehearsal room, the production is an 'unruly ship,' Nikolai says. The actors seem overwhelmed by the onslaught of scenes and, tired, they began to shy away from the magnitude of the piece, 'emoting' vaguely instead of 'performing actions and playing objectives'. After a run of the production on the Monday afternoon, Nikolai calls everyone's attention back to first principles. 'Let's take our time, raise our game, make bold choices and not allow anything to settle.'

Nikolai explains his plan for the week: first, to help the actors acclimatise to the breakneck pace of the production, he asks them to start to consider their 'offstage blocking' as a part of the performance. 'Know where you can drink a glass of water; where someone will be to help you put on a jacket; and where you can focus for two seconds before coming back on. Keep the elastic taut.'

Act 1 runs to eighty minutes, and Nikolai wants it to be no longer than sixty. Act 2 runs to ninety minutes, also too long, although Nikolai is less concerned about that. 'Playing at "the speed of thought" will take off ten minutes,' he says. To the actors playing characters who turn up sporadically in the story, he stresses that whilst a character may not be present in every scene, their journeys are as valid as Pip's. 'Play the time we don't see you,' he says. 'Demand that we follow your journey with as much vitality and rigour as we follow Pip's.'

Before the final few runs in the rehearsal room, Nikolai asks the actors to cast their minds back five weeks to when *Great Expectations* was words on paper. There is little time left before the actors will have to take a backseat to the requirements of the tech. 'There should be nothing niggling as we go into next week,' he says. 'No laments that we could have explored something but didn't.' Before the final run, he entreats the company to 'enjoy performing the play in its purest form' – before technical elements turn it into *A Production*.

By the end of the week, the play is no longer 'bashing around' the company. The final run comes in at a breezy two hours and fifteen minutes. Tanika Gupta, the playwright, attends with Rachel Tackley and Brigid Larmour, the respective artistic directors of English Touring Theatre and Watford Palace Theatre. As the company breaks for the weekend ahead of the tech process, Nikolai thanks everyone in the room for an 'intense, intelligent and lively process so far. It's been difficult and I've learned from working with Tanika and from you all.'

Tech Week ➡

Nikolai sets himself up in the stalls at Watford Palace Theatre, ready for the long haul. I ask him how he is feeling. 'Ask me at lunchtime,' he says. I push the question. 'Sick,' he says. 'That's perfectly normal.'

The actors are standing onstage, looking up into the dress circle, as high as the balcony. Although large, the space feels intimate. Tariq, Simone and Kiran graduated only a few years ago; Lynn remembers playing Watford Palace back in the seventies, and as the stage-management team make the final preparations for the first tech rehearsal, the cast swap stories of past tours and touring life.

Having built a production over five weeks of rehearsal, the company has three-and-a-half days to incorporate the technical elements. 'This week will be tough,' Nikolai says before the tech starts. 'I can't apologise for that. There are many departments working together and they'll throw up challenges all the time. It will seem like no one's listening to you – know that we are. Conserve your energy and look after yourselves.'

They begin at the top of the show. Tariq enters through the auditorium. The house lights fade to black as he reaches the stage. Tariq picks up a pebble (mimed) and skims it out into the auditorium on his left. He follows its movement with his eyes and we hear a faint splash cued in a speaker on the other side of the auditorium. Nikolai directs from the stalls. 'Other side, Tariq.'

The first scene is played behind the cloth. The intention is to create a state reminiscent of a dream. However, the cloth absorbs so much of the ghostly light that shines on it that, halfway back in the stalls, I can only see only silhouettes. Nikolai and Lee, the lighting designer, experiment with different states, finding a medium that allows us to see through the cloth without sacrificing its dreamlike quality. Nikolai is hands-on. He will ask for the light level to raise or lower in a cue by five per cent. He starts, reluctantly, to block actors when their movement rubs against a technical requirement.

The intimacy of the rehearsal room is replaced by the comparative bureaucracy that is tech. Messages are relayed through headphones and microphones and through different crew members, and every instruction takes twice as long to manifest as it did in rehearsal. The process takes its toll on the actors. By the third day, a few of the less experienced actors worry that, in the time it takes to integrate the technical elements of the production, they will have forgotten details of their performances. The older actors implore them to trust the work and themselves. 'It's all in your muscle memory.'

Tensions often run high on at least one day of a production and on the second day of the process, Kate Waters, the fight director, arrives to approve the fight sequences, which have moved from a well-lit rehearsal room to a grittily textured, raked stage in low light, populated by actors holding torches that burn real fire. This is a legal requirement. Kate has been pulled from rehearsals for another production, and travelled by train from central London to Watford. She had assumed that, when she arrived, the company would be ready to work with her, but she finds rehearsals in full swing for another section of the play, and has to wait almost an hour before the production is ready for her. Nikolai is in an impossible position – he cannot stop the tech for her – but he carries the stress of the morning into their first conversation. Already on edge, he goes in hard, declaring upfront that he can't permit any negativity or awkwardness in the room. Kate seems to read this as a presumption that she's going to be difficult. He wants any problems out in the open; she wants to do her job and deal with any politics later. Misunderstandings can happen easily when the stakes are high, people are tired, and your co-workers are talented, forceful people who want their work to be the best it can be. As Nikolai and Kate talk, they realise that they aren't angry with each other so much as the situation. Tempers defuse and Kate climbs on to the stage and starts work with the company. She even adds some new, brutal moves that incorporate the new set.

The day before the production opens, Nikolai is unhappy with the transitions into Miss Havisham's room. The effect is supposed to be ethereal. A curtain is supposed to swoosh past the stage, revealing Miss Havisham as if from nowhere, serene and imperial in her wedding dress and sitting in front of a long table. However, the table is heavy and long, and it rolls on wheels. Nikolai despairs. 'This is the introduction of one of Dickens' most iconic characters and it just looks shit.' It does look shit. The table looks like a contraption and it couldn't be any more conspicuous if it beeped like a van in reverse. What's more, the candles on the table are plastic bulbs, but the audience is close enough to tell. Nikolai wants the table redesigned and the candles changed, which means waiting for the evening.

Nikolai starts to pull rank, partly because there's no time, and partly because he believes in that hierarchy. 'I don't want to get a bad rap because someone else wasn't doing their job,' he says later, after the adrenaline subsides:

> You must never say, 'That will do.' A little part of your heart breaks when you allow yourself to think 'This will be fine, it will be serviceable', because if you do, you're not serving the play that you love. This is a first-class playwright and a brilliant team of actors. Everything you put onstage has to be right, because every decision will be analysed and there is nothing nothing worse than a 'three-star' review.

In tech, the director's responsibility is to the production and he holds that responsibility sacred. However, as the production gets closer to meeting its audience, that responsibility starts to jostle in Nikolai's mind with a responsibility to create a production that he is happy to put his name to. In less than a week, when the production opens, he will walk away and feel as though he has left a beloved child at the school gate. But there is also the practical consideration that another production team and room of actors will soon need one hundred per cent of his attention. 'I want to leave the production safe, with no unfinished business because, if I fail, the actors will be hampered every night,' he says.

Nikolai does not always make it easy on himself. Some directors develop professional personas to survive a world of first nights and being named in the national press, but Nikolai says he has neither the time nor the inclination to do so:

> This job is hard enough without exhausting yourself further by wearing a mask. The person you're talking to right now is the person who you'll have a drink with and who's rehearsing the play. The flip side is that, when something doesn't work, I can get very upset and take it personally. There's no professional defence, and even though we talk about being tough and we drive forwards no matter what, there is a dichotomy. You take things personally and after a few difficult days you think long and hard about whether you said the right thing.

Great Expectations in Performance ➡

Through everyone's hard work, the tech process finishes hours early.

Before the first preview, Nikolai asks the company to battle through any technical problems. 'Be a warhorse,' he says. 'If anything throws you, try to release from it and keep moving. The play must be constantly alive and never settle.'

With the second preview, the cast take a 'huge leap' with Act 2, shaving eight minutes from the running time versus the previous night. 'I know it's crass to talk about time,' Nikolai beams, 'but, *my God*, did you feel it!'

However, in its attempts to power through the second act, the cast has allowed the first act to settle. 'That must never happen,' Nikolai says as he gives notes before the third preview. He asks them to inject some of the rocket fuel they found in Act 2 into Act 1:

> Shake the audience. Force them to engage with you. We approached the play in a cerebral way in rehearsal, but now it's time to put that aside. The subtext is there and the political arguments are there because we've built that into the production. Now it's time to play it and fight your character's corner because there's a lot to fight for, and the more you fight, the more it comes to life.

After three preview performances, Nikolai is able, for the first time, to sit back and enjoy what he has created with the company, and he is struck by the toughness of the world presented onstage. Five weeks ago, on the first day of rehearsals in London, Nikolai had stressed the importance of creating a production that would be more than a version of the novel in miniature. I believed he achieved that.

The Professional ➡️

When we meet a month later, Nikolai affirms his pride in the production: of its ambition in taking an iconic, dense novel that many people feel they 'own', and having the audacity to take it in another direction.

He is, however, ambivalent about the design, which he feels is 'good' but 'not as adventurous as the play' and feels 'too heavy'. 'It's a heavy play,' he says. 'A heavy design hampers that. It's sparse but it's always *there* and it stays *there* no matter where the story moves.' Nikolai is keen to emphasise that he is not blaming the designer (the way he works, the design is very much a collaboration between director and designer). Moreover, he doesn't know what he would do differently, were he and Colin Richmond to have another chance to reinvestigate the design. 'Usually you have an epiphany about a production some time after you leave,' he says. 'That hasn't happened this time.'

In a few days, Nikolai will fly to Singapore to direct a production of *Macbeth*. There will be another script, another company and another set of challenges. He keeps a punishing schedule, which is the only way to scrape a living. 'It's show after show,' he says. 'You have to line them up.' Even having directed a large-scale West End musical, Nikolai's earnings for the previous year will even out to what you'd earn working nine-to-five on minimum wage.

At the same time, that realism, that refusal to fully leave the ground, is part of his success. Commercial theatre has instilled in Nikolai the importance of delivering on time and on budget, and of thinking of himself not only as an artist but as a project manager. Along with his responsibility to writers and actors, he says he is 'beholden' to buildings and the artistic directors who employ him and the producers whose money enables the production.

> If you're going into the industry you should know how to oil the machine – and that means working with producers and it means knowing what a fly-tower is, and how to work with riggers as much as knowing what *mise-en-scène* is.

Nikolai is well-read and he watches many modes and genres of theatre, but he says he has never felt the desire to forge a unique process:

> I have always had four or five weeks' rehearsal, so it's always been about getting on and creating. My process – which is unique, in the way that all our processes are – has stayed because actors seem to like it, and it gets

results. There is a basic shape to how I work, but within that, sometimes you need a circle, sometimes a rectangle. You're responding differently, as an actor does, whether a dream play or a musical or a seventeenth-century romp, so I try to be chameleonic; malleable.

At the age of thirty-one, Nikolai has directed twenty-six professional productions. He speaks with the authority of a man much older, and half-jokes about being an 'old hack'. He talks about the need to reconnect with theatre with the cadence of a man struggling with faith or in love with a difficult partner. 'The business isn't what I thought it was,' he said when we first met in October 2010, reacting to the news that the Culture Secretary Jeremy Hunt would cut almost thirty per cent from the budget of Arts Council England. Nikolai was immediately worried for the education programme at the West Yorkshire Playhouse, a theatre he is closely allied to. 'I fear the next generation will largely be rich kids with the family money to keep creating their own work,' he says. 'Perhaps I should do some teaching. I might teach in a prison, where you can make a difference.' I ask why, if he is so disillusioned, he continues to make work. 'This is my life,' he says, and he means it:

> There are probably other things I could do, but I know I'd be bored. I'm most playful and in touch with my imagination in the rehearsal room. It's a buzz.

> Maybe we keep directing because, if we didn't, we'd feel stifled. The director is an interpretative artist: he shapes the production and makes choices with other artists, and it sounds cheesy, but I feel most like myself in the rehearsal room, creating something then being able to sit in the dark whilst the audience laughs or cries or cheers. That's my bit of private joy.

For better and worse, the most honest, uncluttered version of Nikolai Foster is the version sitting in front of me: the same man you'll find in the rehearsal room.

Carrie Cracknell

Electra

by Nick Payne after Sophocles

The Gate Theatre in association with
the Young Vic

Carrie Cracknell is associate director at the Young Vic and was formerly joint artistic director of the Gate Theatre with Natalie Abrahami (2007–2012), where her productions included *Breathing Irregular*, *Hedda*, *I Am Falling* (also at Sadler's Wells and nominated for a South Bank Show Award in Dance), *Armageddon* and *The Sexual Neuroses of Our Parents*. Other directing credits include *A Doll's House* (Young Vic), *Dolls* (National Theatre of Scotland), *Stacy* (Tron, Glasgow), *A Mobile Thriller* (national tour and Harbourfront, Toronto) and *Broken Road* (British Council Showcase).

'I direct because it's an addiction. Because it never gets any easier. Because when it all comes together – actors, staging, audience, and you get it right – nothing beats it.'

Carrie Cracknell

➤ Cath Whitefield (Electra)

Electra
by Nick Payne after Sophocles

Opened at the Gate Theatre, London, on 7 April 2011.

Creative
Director **Carrie Cracknell**
Designer **Holly Waddington**
Lighting Designer **Guy Hoare**
Music and Sound Designer **Tom Mills**
Movement Director **Georgina Lamb**

Cast
Electra **Cath Whitefield**
Clytemnestra **Madeleine Potter**
Chrysothemis **Natasha Broomfield**
Orestes **Alex Price**
Strophius **Martin Turner**
Young Electra **Yasmin Garrad/Fern Deacon**

The Notion ➡️

The King and Queen of Mycenae, Clytemnestra and Agamemnon, had four children: Electra, Chrysothemis, Orestes and Iphigenia. Agamemnon was a great general in the Greek army, and when his country went to war against Troy, he led the charge. Whilst away, he angered the gods, who demanded as payment that he offer young Iphigenia as a blood sacrifice. Agamemnon lured his wife and child to Troy where he cut Iphigenia's throat. His soldiers' lives were at stake, he said. It was a transaction: one life for thousands. Clytemnestra disagreed. She returned to Greece where she found a lover, Aegisthus, and when Agamemnon returned from Troy, she lured him to the bath with the promise of a relaxing soak and with Aegisthus' help she held him under the water and stabbed him until the water turned red. The King's body was discovered and, in the chaos, Electra smuggled her young brother Orestes out of the palace to an ally of her father's. Electra and Chrysothemis stayed behind. Years passed. Whatever grief Chrysothemis may now feel, she does not articulate it. Meanwhile, Electra incubates her anger, which simmers within her chest. Then, one day, Orestes returns to avenge his father. First, he will kill Clytemnestra, and then he'll kill Aegisthus, just as –

'Woah. Woah. Woah.'

Jenny Worton raises her hand and Carrie Cracknell, the director, stops her recap of the story. 'I'm sorry,' Jenny says. 'The rule is: you kill the biggest baddie last. That's not Aegisthus! The story is about the mother and the children.'

Carrie and Jenny are sitting either side of Carrie's kitchen table opposite Holly Waddington, the designer, and Nick Payne, the writer. The creative team for a new production of *Electra* meets for the first time today and, as a past collaborator of Carrie's, Jenny attends to offer some dramaturgical advice. Right now, her expression seems to ask whether anyone in the room has *ever* seen a horror movie.

The workshop

The story is the myth of Electra as told by Sophocles. Carrie and Holly have presented *Electra* before, in June 2010, in a studio space at the Young Vic: a workshop production that flew under the radar of the national press and gave its tickets away for free. Then, they used a translation of the play by the poet Anne Carson, which stays relatively close to the structure of Sophocles' play.

But although Carrie felt 'playful and unleashed' in directing the movement sections, which involve the chorus, she found other elements of the production challenging. Sophocles' characters often speak to each other in uninterrupted, minutes-long speeches and, to mobilise the text, Carrie struggled to resist directing by 'making beautiful stage pictures', which is to say, 'telling the actors where to stand'. And as she explored the play's many themes – family loyalty, fate, the governance of troubled states – Carrie became drawn to the psychology of its central character, and to the possibility of exploring in more detail the long-term impact of that central, horrific event – Agamemnon's death – on three very different children. She started to develop ideas for a 'cleaner, clearer and more psychologically direct' version of the story for a modern audience.

Soon after, the decision was taken to explore *Electra* in a full production, this time at the Gate, the intimate theatre in Notting Hill that Carrie ran with Natalie Abrahami until early 2012. Carrie decided to commission a new version of *Electra*, one that would inhabit a world of 'epic possibility' that allows for movement and music, but be anchored by psychologically acute acting.

The new writer is Nick Payne, whom Carrie praises for the perceptiveness of his writing about human behaviour, his ear for dialogue and his skill at writing female characters (four of the six characters in the play are women).

Translations and versions

'Translation is always a treason,' Kakuzō tells us in *The Book of Tea*. 'It can at its best be only the reverse of a brocade – all the threads are there, but not the subtlety of colour or design.'

Plays written in another time, or in another language, used to be performed in *translation*. Now, they often appear in *versions* by other playwrights. This distinction can be confusing at first. At its simplest, a translation is the source material rendered scene for scene, most likely in the same socio-historical context, and with its rhythms and images translated as faithfully as the new language allows. Often the translator is an academic or a bilingual playwright fluent in the language of the original.

A version is something freer, which develops the source material. The writer is usually an established playwright, commissioned for the idiosyncrasies of his original work. He may expand or contract themes in the original, although he should do so intelligently, maintaining its identity and dramatic allure.

In approaching *Electra*, Carrie is keen that Nick develops the play, and that the new version, whilst 'still feeling like *Electra*', invites his own artistic contribution.

A new version

Developing the new version, Carrie and Nick are keen to explore the story's motor, which is to say, what is special about today that sets the events of the play in motion. Sophocles' Electra carries her grief for some number of years, but Sophocles does not explore how many, nor does he provide a trigger event that causes Electra's anger to boil over on the day that the action takes place, an issue that most actors and directors, post-Stanislavsky, will want to address. 'I can't say to an actor "You've felt this way for ten years but it's particularly raw today for *some reason*",' Carrie says, as she and Nick discuss what path the new version might take.

Nick's solution is to place the action at the tenth anniversary of Agamemnon's death, which hangs in the air, pressing down on all who live and work in the palace, but most of all on Electra, who has become so disobedient that Aegisthus has convinced Clytemnestra to have Electra 'sent away' from the palace (most likely imprisoned). Nick proposes that the play begins with Aegisthus away from the palace to make the arrangements. Today is Electra's last chance to act.

Aegisthus, for his part, may not feature in the production at all. Sophocles' Aegisthus is discussed by the other characters, but only turns up at the end of the play and is almost immediately killed by Orestes. At the script meeting, Nick wonders aloud if, following the death of Clytemnestra, the death of a character as yet unseen might be less than satisfying. His instinct is that Aegisthus should either be cut entirely, or have his role expanded, perhaps as a terrifying dictator or as a 'sweater-wearing, *Guardian*-reading stepdad' whose only crime, in the children's eyes, is having replaced their father in their mother's affections.

To cut or reconceive a character might be to alter a play fundamentally, and in discussing Aegisthus, Nick and Carrie are mindful of what the play might gain or lose in doing so. Eventually, they decide that Aegisthus is to be cut. The story of *Electra* is old grudges, and Aegisthus is not family.

Also cut is Pylades, Orestes' friend who is present in the first scene of Sophocles' play as Orestes and his tutor arrive at the palace, but does not speak. Orestes' tutor (named by Sophocles for his job, although often transliterated as 'Pedagogus') is given the name Strophius after the ally of Agamemnon who hid the child Orestes on the night of his father's murder.

Workshop ➡

A month before rehearsals begin, Carrie holds a two-day workshop to explore questions that she and Nick have about staging the script. Two of the parts have already been cast. Cath Whitefield will play Electra and Madeleine Potter will play Clytemnestra. Cath and Madeleine attend the workshop with the actor Alison O'Donnell, an 'ally' of Carrie's, who will play whomever else the scene demands.

Carrie articulates her goals upfront, which are, on the day I visit, to explore:

- The effect on the young Electra of witnessing Agamemnon's death.
- The manner of Clytemnestra's death and how much of it (if any) should be depicted onstage.
- The visual vocabulary of the chorus.
- The role of music.

Agamemnon's death

Whilst they have no intention of depicting it in the production, Carrie wants to explore the detail of Agamemnon's death, which happens in a bath tub in a handful of 'awful, crazy seconds' and forms the 'psychological heart of the play'.

The intention is to feed Nick with detail that he may wish to develop in the script, such as the repercussions of different murder weapons: should Agamemnon be shot or stabbed by his killers, who are amateurs, ill-prepared for the job of taking a life? (They settle on a knife, drawn to the physical closeness a stabbing needs versus the distance afforded by a gun.) They try a version in which Agamemnon resists his killers and a version in which he is defenceless, and experiment with how much Electra might see or hear of the event.

The killing is to take place in a bathroom, and as the improvisations develop, it starts to take on a powerful charge that Nick will expand upon, conceiving the bathroom as the room that Electra has, since that day, been scared to go into.

Clytemnestra's death

Sophocles, in keeping with the conventions of his time, does not depict Clytemnestra's death: instead, she is taken offstage by Orestes and the tutor Strophius, and revealed, dead, a few moments later. Nick and Carrie wonder whether to depict the killing, and if so, how much of it.

Carrie is interested in borrowing the editorial tools of sound and light, more often associated with film, and using them to thrust an audience into a world that is 'genuinely frightening' and 'haunted by images of death'. She wants to 'trap the audience and smash things', but as Madeleine's Clytemnestra is dragged, kicking and screaming across the floor to her death, she sits wide-eyed. 'This is horrible,' she says softly. She wonders whether the sequence might be both softened and intensified by choosing a few of its moments to glimpse in light, with the rest happening in darkness to a 'cacophony of scrapes and screams and thuds', and perhaps accompanied by music.

The chorus and the role of music

The traditional Greek chorus is an amorphous group that comments on the action with one, sung voice. In psychological terms, it may be the fractured and often contrary manifestation of Electra's subconscious doubt. Carrie is tempted to explore the possibility that the company, excepting Cath as Electra, also plays the chorus. Today, they develop this idea, exploring what physical laws might govern the chorus, how the actors might transition between embodying the chorus and portraying other characters, and what quality their interactions with Electra might take.

The production's composer, Tom Mills, arrives after lunch with the sheet music to a song that he has drafted to open the production. Tom has set abstract lyrics by Nick to a melody that recalls modern folk music rather than the relentless percussion and chanting incantation that we often hear in classical productions of Greek drama.

First, they treat the song as an underscore, which is how music is often used in films, to simmer under spoken dialogue. Next, they use the music as a foundation of a sequence with movement. Neither approach is entirely satisfying, Carrie says. She feels that unless the music develops from a specific section of the narrative, and has a specific intention, it could feel ostentatious or 'a bit general'. Nick resolves to revisit the lyrics, linking each section of music more explicitly to the passage of text from which it springs.

Pre-rehearsal Development ➡

The design

In the weeks before rehearsals begin, Holly, the designer, continues to explore what the playing space could be, both literally and in what it could present atmospherically and poetically. Carrie and Holly agree that the design should communicate a feeling of confinement and containment that expresses Electra's experience of the palace whilst evoking the deathly images of her dreams.

The final design is a long, thin traverse set that literally represents a foyer in the palace whilst having echoes of the asylum and the abattoir. Under harsh strip lights, its tiled floor takes on an eerie, water-like sheen. Light (designed by Guy Hoare) cuts shafts through smoke. As the performance begins, the door to the auditorium will close, sealing the audience in with the actors.

Electra's arc

Before rehearsals begin with the company, Carrie spends a week with Cath Whitefield at Carrie's house, working on the text and examining some of the character details.

Nick attended when he can. 'You never have enough time for the lead actor,' Carrie says later:

> Electra's journey forms the core of the play, so any work that we can do to clarify that arc before rehearsal means that we can speed up the process proper, and that I will have more time to serve the whole company.

Rehearsals ⟶

The rehearsal building is on an industrial road in Islington, among car-hire firms and small factories. The room itself is a wide, open square, dotted with plug-in heaters. The black paint on its walls is flecked away in Blu-Tack-sized dots where research has been stuck and pulled away, a testament to rehearsal processes past.

Early in her career, Carrie assisted the director Katie Mitchell on her production of Chekhov's *The Seagull* at the National Theatre. Mitchell's philosophy and her approach to working with actors had a strong influence on Carrie's methodology, which she has evolved and developed in different ways.

Carrie's process with actors begins with the principle that performance should be built around 'the clearest, most accurate and truthful set of psychological decisions' about why characters feel and behave as they do, without which, 'all an actor has to go on is blocking or how something "feels"'.

A large part of the rehearsal process, then, is the company working together to get to the heart of what the characters are trying to do to each other and why, and using those discoveries to create a 'solid and robust' basis that will sustain them to experience the story live in each performance.

Script Work ➡️

The company reads the text together. So that everyone is engaged with the process and has a chance to think about every character (not just their own), the parts rotate with each new event (see below). Everyone reads: Carrie reads, Katy, the deputy stage manager reads, I read.

Katy keeps a list of every non-negotiable fact from the world of the play. These facts are mostly information about place, time and action, and give a concrete starting point to the work of rehearsal.

Another list contains every question that the company would like to ask about the world of the play. Questions are not debated round the table, but recorded to be answered at a later date. Carrie assigns some of the questions as homework tasks and so, for the first week, actors present reports on subjects including the scale of the war in Troy, religious beliefs in Ancient Greece, and the possible significance of serpents in dreams.

The two lists become a point of focus to investigate the world, and for the actors to start exploring their characters. Around the third week of rehearsals, every question should have been answered, either collectively through research, through communal decision-making or through biographical character work by the company.

Scene titles

Before rehearsals began, Carrie assigned each of the play's scenes a clear and simple title according to its key event. For example:

Scene 2: *Strophius and Orestes discuss their plan.*

Scene 9: *Chrysothemis discovers that Orestes is dead.*

Where it is hard to name a specific action, Carrie adapts the exercise:

> Scene 3: *The chorus and Electra reflect on her father's death.*

> Scene 5: *The chorus see justice coming.*

The scenes are then subdivided into events.

Events

The process of identifying events and marking them in the script can be a useful tool to break down long sections of text and help actors create psychologically detailed performances, as opposed to performances that feel generalised or overemotional.

A new event occurs when something happens that changes the intention of all of the characters onstage. It could be an action or the introduction of some new information.

Intentions

An intention is a way to describe how characters wish to affect one another. An intention has something active at its heart, and should change with each event. Every character onstage has an intention, whether they speak or not, and should play it to all the characters onstage.

Actions

Actions are specific tactics used to achieve a wider intention moment to moment.

Carrie explains that the aim of using intentions and actions upfront is not to reduce an actor's performance to a set of repeated actions, but to provide a starting point from which he can negotiate the play each night. She does not use the system for each individual line, and encourages actors, should an action go stale through repetition, to reconsider the intention agreed in rehearsal.

Electra is loaded by events in the past, which are known to the characters rather than revealed in the course of the play. Therefore, Carrie adapts the system to help the actors define psychological shifts in their performances, such as when, in the first scene, Electra conjures vivid memories of her father and considers revenge against her mother. Carrie and Cath break down the long sections of text into events that reflect Electra's mind moving between considering the past and the present: remembering, for example, that her father is and always will be dust, then refocusing her attention on the killers, who are at this moment in the same building.

Character Biographies ➡

During the first week of rehearsal, the actors start to piece together a record of their characters' lives. They start with everything that's clear in the text. Where they find gaps, either in the record or in their understanding, they work to fill them in.

Although she does not reveal it to the company, Carrie compiles a spreadsheet that represents each character's age against a line representing the passing years. This lets her see at a glance how old every character was at a certain event, and what time elapses between events. It is only when I look at the spreadsheet that I realise that I had assumed that Clytemnestra's revenge on Agamemnon for sacrificing Iphigenia is almost immediate, when actually *seven years* pass. With this fact, I start to think of Agamemnon's murder not as a crime of passion, but as a premeditated act.

The lists of facts beget questions: for example, it is a fact that Strophius and Orestes arrive at the palace by foot. In rehearsal, the company must decide details such as whether Strophius and Orestes have been to the palace before (perhaps as reconnaissance), and how clear their plan is, including their specific roles in the killing. In one version, they might have planned the operation with military precision; in another, they might be chaotic, fearful and unprepared.

To develop the characters further and to help answer these questions, Carrie leads a process of improvisation.

Improvisation ➡

Fundamentally, improvisation is about 'feeding the actor,' Carrie says. Having improvised the events that lead up to the play, the company can 'walk into a scene for the first time, and it doesn't feel like the first time'. 'We will have met the characters before and in 3D,' she explains. 'When the actors use the material that we generate properly, they will know how their characters communicate and connect with each other.'

There are two stages to the improvisation process. Stage One asks the actors to stage events in their own lives. This is a way to establish shared ground rules about how the company improvises together, and allow it to reflect actively on the themes and emotional ideas of the play.

Stage Two asks the actors to improvise events in their characters' lives as suggested by the lists of facts and questions, and by the character biographies.

So far, the non-actors in the room have contributed to discussion. However, the improvisations will be enacted by the professional actors alone. 'A good improvisation raises everyone's game,' Carrie clarifies. 'Anyone but an experienced actor could lower the standard.'

Three ground rules underpin the improvisation process:

- Don't try to be interesting.
- Don't try to win the audience's sympathy.
- Pay attention to little details about the physical environment.

Stage one: Improvisations on theme

The actors reflect on an event in their past, suggested by a stimulus that Carrie offers. (As rehearsal is not personal therapy, Carrie asks the actors not to draw on traumatic memories.) Groups form, and each is given fifteen minutes to plot the shape of that event whilst leaving room to improvise dialogue. Then the groups share their improvisations and discuss what details they found interesting.

Alex Price (Orestes), teams up with Madeleine (Clytemnestra) to re-enact an argument that Alex had as a teenager with a parent. Carrie directs the discussion towards physical details (how family who are upset with each other might turn their heads away, but not their whole bodies), and comments on how some people in our lives seem always to put us on the defensive, priming us to seek out and amplify criticism. She relates this to Electra's scene with Clytemnestra, in which Electra accuses her mother of 'attacking' and interrupting her as they discuss her father's death.

In another scene, Martin Turner (Strophius) re-enacts with Alex the day that Martin struggled with a test at school, and told his father. The interaction is unmistakably male: emotions bubble under long pauses and what goes unsaid seems to speak as loudly as what is said.

Carrie leads the discussion towards the moment in Orestes' and Strophius's past when Orestes told Strophius that he wants to visit the grave of Agamemnon, his biological father.

Stage two: Improvisations on character

The second stage asks the actors to improvise events in the characters' lives that are not seen in the play. The ground rules are the same, except this time the actors must explain precisely when the event takes place. Carrie asks that the actors not concern themselves with stagecraft or even think about an audience, as an actor in performance might.

Carrie has prepared the first scenarios in advance. Soon, she will invite suggestions from the company.

The first improvisation explores the three children – Electra, Orestes and Chrysothemis – as children (twelve, eight and nine years old, respectively), as they play together in the palace grounds. Agamemnon is still alive, although he is fighting in Troy, and only Electra remembers him with any clarity. She tells stories of her father whilst Orestes plays war with sticks and stones.

After the improvisation is shared, Carrie stimulates the actors by asking questions. She asks Cath (Electra) whether Electra, being the eldest child, might feel responsible for her siblings; and did she support and encourage them or boss them around? Watching Alex's Orestes play war, she wonders whether Orestes might have pent-up aggression and whether he wants to be impressive for when his father returns.

Over the next days, they enact scenarios including:

- The first time Strophius told Orestes about his father's death.

- A dinner party with the whole family that Electra disrupts.
- Clytemnestra brushing her daughter Chrysothemis's hair and talking about Electra, who is not present.

Carrie says that an improvisation is useful when it helps a company understand a play – as the playwright wrote it. An improvisation is therefore unhelpful if, instead of fuelling the action, it takes an actor further from the text. This happens one afternoon when, improvising a discussion between Strophius and Orestes about the possibility of killing Clytemnestra, Martin's Strophius takes such a strong lead that Orestes becomes almost an instrument of his will. When the scene ends, Carrie asks Alex to reconsider the elements of the play that led him to make those connections.

Before this stage of the process ends, Carrie asks the actors to think whether there are any other scenes in their characters' lives that they would like to improvise. Although the process ends formally, she will return to improvisation throughout, when a particular moment or area of the play seems unclear.

Movement ➡️

For the first week of rehearsals, the company works at the table throughout the morning and explores character through improvisation and movement in the afternoon.

Georgina Lamb, the production's movement director, leads her first session with the company late in the first week. She leads games to bond the cast, dissolve any lingering barriers to physical closeness and introduce the language of the amorphous, non-individuated identity that is the Greek chorus. Carrie sits and observes. She takes the opportunity to observe and consider the company as a whole. Nick Payne is on the other side of the room, tapping away at his laptop, refocusing parts of the script in response to discoveries made during the improvisation process.

I watch as the company becomes the chorus, a morphing character that collectively represents Electra's emotional state and characters in her life as she perceives them. As Electra, Cath starts to interact with the chorus. She moves and it follows at a fractional delay. It seems to hunt her; it seems to be questioning her. She walks towards it, and it seems to become liquid around her, then glass that shatters at her touch.

Carrie wants to articulate the terror of the child, frightened in a big house, unsure of who to trust and struggling to move beyond a traumatic event. Under her direction, the chorus develops motifs that resonate with Electra's story. I watch as the chorus coalesces into a number of images of a lonely child: it stands in the corner, its head pressed to the wall; it plays hide-and-seek on its own; it revisits the moment Electra found her father dying in the bathroom. As Carrie watches, she takes notes, sketching, as a designer might, images that resonate with her, that she might plant in the story.

Having developed a vocabulary for the chorus, rehearsal turns to the opening scene of the play, which is a movement sequence with music. Tom Mills, the production's composer, plays the music from the piano.

The performance begins with the auditorium doors slamming closed, sealing the audience in with the actors. The chorus sings of a city in decline, burdened by loss and commenting on the cruelty of fate. Electra, it sings, is 'not one to forget' nor 'one to be forgotten'.

Watching the rehearsal, Nick goes into 'dramaturg mode'. He feels the sequence is trying to achieve too many objectives. 'At the beginning of a play, the audience is taking in the space and the actors,' he says. 'We're trying to tell a lot of story *and* establish the chorus *and* establish that members of the chorus double as other characters. There's so much to take in, I'm not sure any of it will land.' Tom, at the piano, agrees. Carrie suggests halving the song but Nick wants to go further; he wants to distill the sequence to a single image that could be titled: 'There has been an event that Electra cannot forget.' The rest, he says, should be humming, not lyrics. He writes in the margin of his script, 'new lyrics', underlines it twice and immediately starts sketching ideas. A few days later, the opening is reworked into a shorter movement section without lyrics.

Electra and Orestes ➡

Two weeks in, the company rehearses the scene in which Electra meets her brother Orestes, who has arrived at the palace disguised as a messenger. He carries a box in which he says are the ashes of Orestes, who has drowned. When he sees the depth of Electra's grief, he reveals his true identity.

It is an emotional scene: within minutes, Electra experiences extreme grief followed by elation, followed by the realisation that Orestes has returned to kill their mother.

Instead of commenting on the emotional 'depth' of a moment and asking an actor to be arbitrarily 'sadder' or 'happier', Carrie directs by refining or changing intentions and tactics. Instead of directing the actors to manufacture the outward signs of emotion – 'smile', 'look sad' – she asks them to keep vivid certain 'imagined pictures' to trigger the emotions spontaneously. For example, Carrie directs Cath to harness the idea that the box in Orestes' hands contains everything that is left of her brother. 'To hand the box back to this stranger is to lose him all over again,' she says, and suggests that Cath simply try to hold on to the box for longer when Alex asks for it back. In turn, she approaches the script's demand that Orestes and Electra make enough noise that Strophius has to enter from next door to shut them up, not by asking the actors to 'be louder', but by asking Alex to keep at the front of his mind an awareness of how close the palace guards must be, and the knowledge that every minute they spend in the palace increases their chance of being caught. She then suggests to Cath that Electra might focus on recalling the night Orestes left. They enact the scene again. Orestes is playing two things: there is his awareness of the guards, which brings a heightened sense of place and tension, and the intensity of his emotion towards his long-lost sister. Then there is Electra, holding what she thinks are the ashes of her dead brother, and feeling she has lost him all over again. Her expression of that guilt fuels Orestes, and vice versa, until the volume builds and brings Strophius out of the palace.

Rumble-through

At the end of the third week of rehearsals, the company runs the show for the first time. The first run of a production is inherently tentative, and so it is often called a 'stumble-through'. Carrie prefers the term 'rumble-through' (or 'rumble' for short). To stumble is to 'trip or momentarily lose one's balance; almost fall'. But a rumble, however scrappy, is a fight you intend to win.

The rumble alerts the cast to the intensity of the production. Once the doors to the auditorium close, they are visible for the entire performance. The strain on Electra to anchor the performance feels more acute than ever. Cath invests in every scene and is exhausted by the end. 'I can't let the ball drop, can I?' she says. The chorus, for its part, must support her by re-energising the space with its every entrance.

Before the company breaks for the weekend, Carrie asks if anyone has any 'profound anxieties' that might plague them all weekend, or anything they want her to think about for Monday.

The Gate ➡

Because design is an integral part of the production, the final two weeks of rehearsal are held on set in the venue.

Digging

In the workshop production, Carrie and Holly explored a staging idea in which Electra took a spade and dug deep into the earth. It happened in the moments after Electra hears of Orestes' death, and after her sister Chrysothemis tells her, categorically, that she will not be a part of any plan to hurt their mother. Carrie feels that, as a 3D expression of the world of the play, the moment was one of the most exciting and successful of that production, and she has been keen to develop it with Nick.

At the Gate, Holly's team has raised the auditorium floor by sixty centimetres, allowing them to build a pit centre stage, which they hide with the same tiles that cover the floor. Alone, Electra seems to hear a noise from beneath the floor. She smashes the tiles and rips up the floor, pulling out support beams and heaping dirt onto the floor around her before lying in the pit she has dug – for herself? For Orestes? For her mother? – where she sings a song condemning her enemies' 'deceitful speech' and imploring the memory of her father: 'Do not stay silent, do not withdraw from me.'

Carrie and Nick discuss whether the chorus should be present, and whether the sequence should be framed as a kind of ritual, perhaps with the chorus laying tea lights on the ground. Nick resists the idea. 'The act of breaking the floor is massive,' he says. 'We already have the visual image of Electra digging furiously then lying in a grave, covered in dirt, surrounded by cracked tiles and singing a song. Is it too much to have tea lights as well?'

The discoveries of rehearsal distill the sequence further. The music that Tom has recorded for Cath to sing over is cut and so she sings unaccompanied. In the final production, Cath will dig for almost two minutes without speaking. The only sounds will be her grunting and crying, and the sound of spade on earth.

Clytemnestra's murder

To be allowed to turn off every light in a theatre requires special permission from the council. For *Electra*, even the emergency and exit lights are disabled to enact the sequence in which Orestes and Strophius kill Clytemnestra. The murder will happen in complete darkness, with light flaring up for a second at a time to glimpse the most extreme moments.

The team tests the effect. There is only inky blackness. As Katy, the stage manager, walks offstage to where she will cue the lights – a monitor fed by an infrared camera allows her to see – her torch flashes around the space, its light glancing off the pit, which is open from the morning's rehearsals. We glimpse a spade on its side, shards of wood, piles of dirt. The room is a crime scene. A tomb.

The sequence is conceived moment by moment, from the killers' imperative to immobilise their victim and her goal to escape, through to her appeal to her son, on grounds of family, to stop, to her desperate fight for life, through to her plea for a quick death. The killers experience moments of doubt and fear as Orestes struggles to follow through or gets carried away, tempted for a moment to tear out Clytemnestra's eyes. When the lights rise and Clytemnestra's body is revealed in the pit, Orestes is giddy with aggression and has nowhere to channel it. Possibly, he is in shock.

The sequence is complex. In total darkness, Alex (Orestes) must chase Madeleine (Clytemnestra) across the pit, around soil and broken tiles, and into Martin's (Strophius's) path. He will slam her head into the floor, stab her and drag her body into the dirty pit, where Madeleine must apply fake blood to her head before the lights rise to reveal the aftermath.

Coordinating the movement is not easy, and the sequence is modified for safety whilst retaining its psychological grounding. For example, instead of the lights flaring up as Orestes plunges his knife into Clytemnestra, the lights will rise as he pulls the knife out of her body.

Tech

Tech is 'probably my favourite part of rehearsal,' Carrie says:

> Tech and previews are the real test. It's when a lot of directing happens. You have the raw material – the structure – and you can hone and perfect, moment by moment. It's exciting if you can be bold in that period and sustain your energy.

As she evolves the work with the creatives, Carrie seems to be more forthcoming and plain-spoken than she might be with the actors. She might describe a sequence or an idea as having 'a massive hole in it' or decide that a moment that is holding up the session should be 'put it on the list' to re-examine later. I observe that with the creative team, Carrie will talk of the need to 'fix' or 'solve' a cue, which are words she has not used with the actors. I ask her when she knows a cue has been 'fixed' or 'solved', and she drops her voice to a conspiratorial, too-quiet-for-the-microphone whisper:

> You don't, really. You *never* do! The challenge of tech is to make the process creative for everyone, not just the creative team. It's unfortunate that tech has to be the last thing a production does before it opens, because actors can feel it's an uncreative process for them, but you must treasure that time because the creative team are doing something that is profoundly difficult and exposing: they are creating material live in front of everybody and they need the chance to fuck up. You must protect that time, because you only have tech and previews to make the work brilliant – once the run starts proper, they leave. With actors, we're building a basis for them to stay live and grow in depth and variety. The language with the actors is about longevity. Your time with the creative team is compressed.

Grasp the Nettle ➡

On the second day of the tech, Carrie takes a bold decision. The cast assembles in the auditorium and Carrie breaks the news that the chorus is to change.

The third draft of the script, written before rehearsals began, introduced an idea that will become one of the production's defining images. As he wrote the earlier drafts, Nick Payne immersed himself in books about the science of childhood trauma, which taught him among other things that children often experience profound guilt at not having been able to intervene in the death of a parent, even if they were too young to stop it. Nick posited that Electra witnessed her father's death, whereas Chrysothemis didn't. Electra's relationship to the event is therefore 'very different' to her sister's.

The idea had excited the team, and a conversation with Holly Waddington, the designer, unlocked for Carrie the idea of including within the chorus a young girl who represents Electra on the night of her father's murder: a manifestation of a mind stuck in the past. Played by a child actor, Young Electra could be a part of the chorus that splits from the group and whom Electra addresses directly. Nick embraced the idea, including Young Electra as a named character in the script.

As the production developed, Young Electra took a more central role, and seeing the production working in the Gate, Carrie started to feel that the chorus as imagined so far, might not be the most interesting solution. 'Having seen the chorus working in the Gate itself,' she says, 'I've been able to clarify what I want the production to articulate, and the most interesting element of the chorus is Electra being caught at the moment her father died. That's come to drive our vision.'

Earlier in her career, she would have waited until previews to make such a change, but faced with the prospect of spending a day of integrating light and sound with action that she knew would be cut eventually, she resolved to do it now.

She explains her reasons to the cast, and that her mind is made up, then calls a break. 'You can have a smoke and a bitch,' she says. 'Does anyone need a punchbag?' Outside, she gathers her thoughts. 'You have to have one day like this. Sometimes it's ten days – it depends on the show. I have a new mantra: grasp the nettle. It's brutal, possibly, but when you're in tech, you have to think economically about time.'

To change the chorus means removing swathes of Tom Mills's music, and much of Georgina Lamb's contribution to the production, although their presence is embedded in the production's DNA. The other big repercussion is that, two days before it opens to the public, the production no longer has an opening sequence. Carrie is ready to work on a new sequence that, like Clytemnestra's murder, will play to music and is glimpsed in flashes of light. Some of the images will return in some form later in the performance, such as Clytemnestra haunted as if in a horror movie by the image of someone behind her. Young Electra will be seen running through the palace (perhaps in the moments before she finds her father in the bath, and squaring off against her older self), planting the connection between Electra and Young Electra, and setting up the rule that the girl represents Electra at a point in time.

Dress Rehearsal ⟹

'The dress rehearsal can be calm,' Carrie says. 'It needn't be a panic if the director manages the journey from tech to dress.' She supports the company in its transition to performance by managing expectations, telling the cast that the dress will be 'scrappy' and that they should use the time to adjust to each new element, and arranging a 'home crowd' of the Gate's volunteer box-office staff and ushers.

Carrie's notes that evening are a combination of small fixes and thoughts about wider characters arcs. She reminds the actors to remember to 'place in their minds the *imagined pictures* and sense of *setting*'. Performing for the first time with every technical element in place is almost always destabilising for a company, and the actors appear particularly grateful for practical notes. 'More volume in Scene 3,' Carrie says to Cath, who nods and takes a pen to the margin of her script.

Electra in Performance ⟹

After the first preview, Carrie and Nick Payne, the playwright, share a minicab back to their homes on the other side of London. As they travel, they discuss the fundamentals of the story. They decide to reinforce some of its basic elements for audience members who aren't familiar with Greek mythology, such as who Agamemnon was to the Greek army. The next morning, Nick writes new material whilst Carrie assembles the cast onstage.

She reflects that 'the skeleton of the show feels clear and strong':

> We're still feeding the show and the main area of
> evolution now is trying to tweak corners that help us
> clarify the journey. The preview period is about making

> the story as clear and compelling and truthful as
> possible. We're working live with technical elements and
> performance to bring the show out to be the strongest
> version of itself. We're still feeding the show –
> deepening the work and developing the acting.

Until press night, the company assembles each day at 1:30 p.m. and works until five p.m., tightening the material and evolving technical cues. There are small fixes, such as repositioning Madeleine in the killing sequence so that her breathing isn't noticeable after Clytemnestra has died, and making Electra a more prominent witness to the event. Carrie spends an hour with Cath and Natasha (Chrysothemis) on their key scene together, reinforcing and building on their work they did in rehearsal on the bickering, sisterly quality of their relationship.

Watching *Electra* in performance, Nick gains clarity that helps him edit the text. The day after the second preview, Nick suggests a number of revisions and cuts, which the company rehearse. The published script, which went to print towards the end of rehearsals and is displayed proudly in the foyer, now differs significantly from the play as performed. Nick shrugs. 'That always happens.'

The largest cut is the entire last page of the script. At the end of the play, the remaining characters are assembled around Clytemnestra's corpse. Chrysothemis fails to close her mother's eyes, and collapses in Electra's arms, who rocks her ever so gently. Electra tells Chrysothemis not to look at the wounds – 'It's the only way to stop the bleeding' – and, as the sun begins to creeps over the horizon, the play ends. The ending is relatively peaceful. However, Carrie and Nick are eager to emphasise the idea, discussed before rehearsals started, that violence is often a cycle. The ending is shortened: Chrysothemis asks what Orestes and Strophius intend to do with

Aegisthus. Orestes replies, 'We're going to kill him' – and the lights plunge to black.

The fourth preview is a little scratchy. Tired by the intensity of the work, and of juggling the demands of remembering so many small changes, there are a few late entrances, and physical confusion, with a few actors stumbling around the pit and even slipping on the stairs. Carrie adjusts the next day's schedule to give the company more time to practise the changes. 'It's important to keep riding through,' she says. 'Keep the energy up. Keep live to each other.'

After the production opens, Carrie attends each week of the run to give notes. Whilst there is less time after press night to reinvestigate the production, she believes it is important that the last matinee should have the depth and intensity of the press night. 'Ideally, it should be better,' she says. 'It should keep growing.'

Clarity and Strength ➡

Early in the project, Carrie and Nick discussed whether the attempt would be a version of Sophocles' *Electra*, a freer adaptation, or even an original play about matricide. The production that opened was a conversation between a new play and an old play. Nick observed the precision of Sophocles' structure where it helped him, including its Aristotelian unity of time and place, whilst developing the dialogue, the music, and, in conversation with Carrie, the role of the chorus. What stays with me about the production is the mix of its visceral aesthetic and the intimacy of the writing, which feels less a play about kings, queens and the throne of Mycenae, and more a play about a mother, two daughters and a son.

I meet Carrie shortly after *Electra* closes at the Gate. She is proud of the production and of Nick, whose version of the story she feels is 'extraordinary'. The reviews were mixed, with some critics feeling that the version went too far in adapting the source material. Carrie reads the reviews. To refuse to, she says, is 'a bit perverse, even childish':

> Criticism is the prism through which we witness work, and it impacts sales massively, which you're especially aware of if you run a building and so have a duty of care to your staff – financially, artistically. But every director has that responsibility to the company. If your production receives a particularly difficult write-up, then it's your responsibility to do what you can to protect the company; to make that phone call or have that cup of tea with an actor and help them from doubting themselves, and know that the choices they made are clear and relevant to the production.

Carrie expects the cast to feed back the conversation about how the work is evolving, and in turn she relies on a close circle of trusted advisors. Those people should be the creative team plus a few long-term collaborators, she says; people to whom you can say: ' "I think I'm following my instincts and I think I'm judging accurately but can you double check? Is there anything I've missed?" It's empowering to know who to take those notes from and who not to take them from.' The opinion of a director's partner also 'matters massively,' she says.

Carrie's process, at least as observed in *Electra*, appears fairly regimented, progressing through stages. It is also idiosyncratic and highly expressive of a strong, personal aesthetic and emotional reality. Indeed, the most unique directors, Carrie says, tend to be those whose work expresses their emotional world and their interests and their aesthetic, rather than just serving a text. Carrie often teaches emerging directors and is most excited when she feels that she understands a director's creative identity:

> Some people come to the meeting and you think: '*Bam!* I know who you are. I know what job I might offer you and what you could offer my building.' Other people come in and tell me they like 'this and that' and they could be any other person, so why offer them the job? I think the key is to find out for yourself what kind of work you really want to make, what you want to say, and find a way to define that and then learn how to express it.

We talk about careers, and about training for emerging directors. A career as a theatre director has a number of 'ledges', she says: different moments when a person can lose their footing. The first ledge usually comes when a student is leaving university, she says. They will have made a few productions that excited people, and someone sees one and offers the director the chance to assist someone more established. 'I always say to people: assist now,' Carrie says. 'If you miss that step, you can't go back. I can't assist now – people wouldn't let me – and there are people I'd bite off my arm to be in the room with.'

The director who advances past the first ledge faces a tougher climb. More emerging directors fall down the gap between being seen as an assistant and being seen as a creative talent in one's own right. Carrie has employed many assistants, and she understands the frustration of the director who feels that, after studying at drama school and assisting however many directors, she is 'owed' a production of her own and wonders why the phone isn't ringing. 'The answer is: because no one has seen your work; therefore, we have no idea who you are,' Carrie says. 'If you have only assisted, then the production didn't originate with you, and you have never run a room of your own. You need to have a strong idea of your own – something that makes you stand out – and deliver that vision onstage.'

She advocates a similarly 'tough-love' approach for emerging directors who are afraid that, after 'ten or so shows on the fringe', their careers are stalling:

> Hold back. Save up all your ideas and all your money, and do one thing and *nail* it. Raise enough money or save enough money to secure a good lighting designer and a good set designer, and find someone to design a beautiful flyer. If you don't have the money for twelve actors, then do a show with two; something that shows that you know how to work with a writer and with actors and that you can do something classy for little money. That's all you need. Then, people can't *not* employ you!

Carrie's aesthetic sensibility has been with her, she says, since she was a student, although it has refined and deepened from its core. The way she manages people has always been 'instinctive', she says, inherited from her mother. What has developed are the skills to help actors create the kind of work she is interested in. She recalls, as a student director, asking an actor playing Lady Macbeth to 'try to deepen her performance a bit'. Recalling the event, Carrie's eyes widen at her naivety. 'I didn't have a clue when I started,' she says. 'The process of discovery has been learning how to articulate clearly what I want and enable actors to get to a specific performance. You have to learn those tools.'

Ultimately, what makes a director is her instinct, she says. 'Everyone's approach and belief and taste is different. All you can do is keep coming back to what you believe and what you find exciting and strong and clear.'

Joe Hill-Gibbins

The Glass Menagerie
by Tennessee Williams
Young Vic

Joe Hill-Gibbins is deputy artistic director of the Young Vic. Directing includes *The Changeling*, *The Beauty Queen of Leenane* and *A Respectable Wedding* (Young Vic); *The Village Bike*, *Bliss*, *Family Plays* and *A Girl in a Car with a Man* (Royal Court); *The Girlfriend Experience* (Young Vic and Royal Court/Drum Theatre, Plymouth); *The Fever* (Theatre503 in association with the Young Vic); and *A Thought in Three Parts* (James Menzies-Kitchin Award-winner, BAC 2002).

'Directing is highly personal, yet completely collaborative. We're sometimes told that having a particularly strong emotional reaction to something in a play could blind us, but as long as it's coupled to rigorous analysis... that's the point, isn't it?'

Joe Hill-Gibbins

Leo Bill (Tom Wingfield)

The Glass Menagerie
by Tennessee Williams

Opened at the Young Vic, London, on 11 November 2010.

Creative
Director **Joe Hill-Gibbins**
Designer **Jeremy Herbert**
Costume Designer **Laura Hopkins**
Music **Dario Marianelli**
Lighting Designer **James Farncombe**
Sound Designer **Mike Walker**
Choreography **Arthur Pita**
Video Creation **Steve Williams**
Casting **Julia Horan**
Dialect Coach **Michaela Kennen**

Cast
Tom Wingfield **Leo Bill**
Amanda Wingfield **Deborah Findlay**
Laura Wingfield **Sinéad Matthews**
Jim O'Connor **Kyle Soller**

The Wingfields of St Louis ➡

The Wingfield family – mother Amanda, son Tom, daughter Laura and their father, long gone but whose presence is ever-felt – might be the most famous dysfunctional family of American theatre. Holed up in a shoebox apartment in St Louis, Missouri, the closest they come to privacy is afford by curtains that subdivide the tiny space still further. Mother resents son for his inability to grow up; son resents mother for the menial job he endures to support her and his sister. And between them is Laura. Unapproachably shy and plagued by a limp, Laura opts out of life, escaping instead into a fantasy world where she is caretaker and confidante to a table of glass animals. Everyone wants out.

The play is *The Glass Menagerie* by Tennessee Williams, in a new production at the Young Vic by its deputy artistic director, Joe Hill-Gibbins. 'The most interesting plays,' Joe says:

> are about irresolvable, often painful contradictions in human nature: things you can turn over in your mind a thousand times, even struggle with your whole life, but never resolve. Weaker plays might take a moralistic view of the world, aligning characters' actions and motivations to clear right and wrong. That might not necessarily be a bad way to look at the world, but it's a weak starting point for drama.

The Glass Menagerie contains neither heroes nor villains. The characters' decisions, compelled by their situation and by internal conflicts, are difficult to criticise. The play is framed by its narrator, Tom, who is writing to access painful memories about his sister and mother whom he abandoned years ago, shortly after he agreed to find a potential husband – a 'gentleman caller' – for Laura, and inadvertently created a disaster. To watch Tom struggle to make sense of those events is to watch Tennessee Williams ask perhaps the ultimate question for a theatremaker: why do we make plays?

The fact that you cannot identify the one 'right' action that a character should have taken is, Joe argues, a component of powerful dramatic writing. For each character to flourish, they must leave behind a life that has become a trap, yet they cannot, for their fates are entangled. 'Tom cannot be who he is – he cannot discover his identity, in writing or in life – whilst he remains in that house with his mother and sister,' Joe observes. 'He has to leave. The contradiction is: he can't leave his family without leaving them destitute.' And so we 'tear the family apart onstage' whilst knowing that the tensions within them have no answer.

The Memory Process →

We are sitting in the staff break room at the Young Vic. It is a Saturday morning in August, a few hours before a matinee performance of Joe's revival of *The Beauty Queen of Leenane* by Martin McDonagh, which has returned after a successful run a year before.

Joe opens his laptop and navigates to a folder of photographs from the design and rehearsal processes for *The Glass Menagerie*, which closed six months before.

This chapter is a little different. Elsewhere, I was in rehearsal with the company. Here, I was part of a workshop team that helped explore the creative team's early ideas for the production, but I did not attend rehearsals for the production proper. Six months later, after the production closed, we are reconstructing the process from memory and notes.

The photos kickstart Joe's memory. There are hundreds: he takes photographs at a furious rate, whenever an arrangements of bodies or objects in space looks interesting or mysterious or in some way dramatic. A few minutes ago, we were in the Maria, the larger of the Young Vic's two studio spaces, and Joe photographed a toolbox near to a stack of chairs and rows of steeldeck, left by a technician on break. He shows me the picture on his phone. 'It looks like a set, designed by chance,' he says. In rehearsal, chance might arrange the actors onstage in some configuration that resembles a painting, or has some significance to be untangled later and he will take a photo, which is something instinctual, perhaps to be analysed or recreated later, or not. 'It's a way of aestheticising life,' he supposes.

Aestheticising life seems also to encapsulate the role of a theatre director, and is a theme of the play at hand.

The Memory Play ➡️

The Glass Menagerie was revolutionary when it premiered in 1944 and has remained a cornerstone of twentieth-century American theatre. Its domestic naturalism is embellished and exaggerated by poetic and expressionist elements such as music that comes from outside the story space, narration by Tom, and captions and photographs projected over the action onto gauze. Published copies of the play are prefaced with a set of production notes by the author that explain 'the screen device' (the gauze) and the role of lighting within the play. In that sense, Williams is not only writing a play but a manifesto for a type of theatre, and so he defines the terms of engagement. Before he can interpret the material, Joe must understand what Williams wanted *The Glass Menagerie* to achieve. 'At the start of the play,' Joe says, 'Tom Wingfield walks onstage and tells the audience that he is going to present the story of his family. In that moment, Tennessee Williams invents the memory play,' Joe observes. 'We might think of *The Glass Menagerie* as an old-fashioned, "well-made play". The reality is that the piece is very fragmented.'

British theatre is historically writer-led and permeated with the suggestion that a creative team should 'just do the play', and that a director, if he only concentrated 'harder' on the text, could distill from it some singular production. 'This is bollocks,' Joe says. 'There are complex choices to make at every stage.' There would be even if a production adhered to every last stage direction. Joe cites the model of his frequent collaborator Zoë Svendsen, a director, translator and researcher, in which the director is invited to imagine the play as a spider's web with strands emanating from the centre: the author's life, the various themes and settings. At some point, the creative team must decide where to place their spider on that web.

The First Workshop
(or The Story of the Portières) ➡

To explore some of the questions raised by his research into the play, Joe decides to hold a workshop. A director's most important creative relationship is with his designer, Joe says:

> The process is exhaustive and takes a long time so it should start as soon as possible. Find the right person and go hell-for-leather to get them on-board.

On this production, the right person is Jeremy Herbert. *The Glass Menagerie* is Jeremy and Joe's second collaboration.

Long before the rehearsal period, Joe and Jeremy want to work through the play, in 3D and fast, building up and tearing down sets made from whatever objects are nearby. To help, they gather a team from within the Young Vic's Directors Programme, which incubates emerging directors and offers opportunities for development.

On the first day, Joe emphasises the importance of questioning the script as a principle. He cites the mantra of the Russian director Lev Dodin, that the director who reads a text and does not at the end have a thousand questions cannot be paying enough attention.

Having read the play together, the group divides into teams to draft a design for the Wingfield apartment that follows the opening stage directions. The group votes on a winner and builds that design from steeldeck and whatever else it can find. Following Joe's instruction, the group builds fast. The portières, which subdivide the living space, are represented by a flipchart and a wastepaper bin. The portrait of the father, which looms over the apartment, is sketched in marker pen on the side of a box.

© 2010 Joe Hill-Gibbins

The first 'design'

The group works through the play, redesigning the set scene by scene, adding and taking away based on what the stage directions describe. If, for example, the portières aren't referred to or touched during a scene, they are removed. The group might have decided that the winning design was 'the right way' to stage the play, and spent a week exploring the play within that space. Instead, it explores different shifts of emphasis, and stays receptive to discoveries. Indeed, the early days of the workshop are a quantum event of multiple productions that exist in multiple universes simultaneously, with Joe at the centre, questioning and provoking until he might decide where on the web to place the spider.

Looking at the play in 3D, Joe realises how the geography of the apartment, and its use by the characters, resembles a theatre stage. The sitting room and dining area seem to divide neatly into forestage and backstage, with the portières acting as a theatrical curtain. Watching the group perform the first scene, in which Tom and Amanda argue over dinner, Joe becomes attuned to the ways in which the characters appear to be in a performance. There is Amanda, for whom dinnertime is an opportunity to perform the rituals of the fondly remembered South, and Tom the sulky actor who refuses to comply with his 'director' and walking offstage. Most of the second act is a performance by the Wingfields with elaborate costumes, props, and a rebelling actor, put on to impress the gentleman caller. That *The Glass Menagerie* is 'a hymn to the theatre', as Joe says, is clear. The Wingfields are performers of sorts who use fantasy to make their reality bearable: Tom by writing fiction or consuming cinema, where, the subtext tells us, he cruises for sex. (He does that so often that it becomes a laugh line in the play.) Laura has the glass menagerie and Amanda has the past. But the match between form and content, and the notion of make-believe are becoming clearer and will come to power the production.

Joe said at the start that he was loathe to present 'the boring version of the play', which would explore theatricality by having Tom step out of an otherwise naturalistic set every time he delivers a monologue. (Search online for 'Glass Menagerie set'. You'll see many of those.) The exploration of theatricality must go deeper than 'reminding the audience that they're in a theatre'. That alone is, Joe says 'an empty exploration' ('and *really*... so what?'). The production must find a way to express in the design something deeper. Something more linked to character. Something... *else*. Something unknown as yet, for the design develops in 'little fragments' rather than in a 'big bang'.

The Aesthetics of Escape ➡

In the weeks that follow, the production develops at speed. Buoyed by the discoveries of the workshop, Jeremy collects hundreds of photographs of the ornate cinemas of the 1930s that Tom would have frequented, which were, perhaps ironically, theatres converted after the arrival of film.

Returning to the Young Vic, they start to consider the difference between these ornate theatres and the workmanlike auditorium during the day when the house lights are on. Two competing and contrasting aesthetics begin to emerge: the aesthetic of the theatre, with its metal walkways, exposed steeldeck and brick walls, and the act of transformation when light sweetens a red curtain or dances off a mirror ball. There is the Brechtian, exposed theatre of harsh, Depression-era life, and the consumptive, glamorous theatre of escape. This dichotomy comes to symbolise, for Joe and Jeremy, the characters' attempts to transcend reality through make-believe and rose-tinted memories. As Joe explains:

> The goal is to use the formal elements of theatre to express the story. If we choose to take a dressing-room unit from the Young Vic dressing rooms and have Amanda change clothes onstage, we aren't doing it to say 'Look, we're in a theatre', but to point out that Amanda dresses up to perform roles, whether it's a dinner or to play the respectable lady from the Daughters of the American Revolution [an elite social club]. It helps tell the story.

A few months later, with rehearsals due to start in a month, Joe holds a second workshop, this time with a smaller group.

The Second Workshop ➡

On day one, the group goes back to the text, exploring Tennessee Williams's screen device, on which captions and photographs are projected that comment on the story. The group create rough-and-ready slides on a laptop plugged into a projector and run a version of the show that includes every title card and musical cue that Williams prescribes. In 1944, when the play premiered, gauze was a new technology. A modern creative team can, of course, project onto almost any surface, and can project moving images. The exercise allows Joe and Jeremy to see how the action differs when played in 3D with visible captions, and which of the illustrations, if any, they might carry through to the production.

Next, the team builds a set in which each character has a space to call their own: Laura has a hideaway tucked up in the corner of the lounge area, which she makes from sofa cushions and bedsheets; Tom gets a writer's retreat at the dining-room table; Amanda receives a bedroom decorated with trinkets from her antebellum past. But once the scenes begin, the characters become locked in their silos. The space is many things: an apartment in St Louis, a theatre, and the inside of a man's mind. Because the play comprises scenes from Tom's memory, the space must be fluid: it must reconfigure in time and space, and in response to the intensity of his recollection. Joe starts to feel that he is contriving reasons to get the actors moving and active in each other's spaces. The design also feels 'freeze-dried', he says, 'too much like a schematic.' He asks aloud, 'What is the *idea* at work?'

By now, Jeremy has experimented not only with the projections, but with five versions of the portières alone, and a version where neither the glass menagerie nor the fire escape are represented onstage. Later, I will suggest to Joe that the story of the production became the story of its design. 'Yes and no,' he will say. 'You have to understand that design is not only about "a set"; it's about everything. It's about how the production *works*.' At the first workshop, Joe said that 'direction is design and design is direction'. He elaborates to explain that whilst a design should 'exploit and play with the formal qualities that are particular to theatre to express story and characterisation', it is also, on a practical level, the space for actors to inhabit. The nuts and bolts of where a designer places a door, for example, carries an abstract weighting. To illustrate his point, Joe highlights the difference between a person storming out of a room by walking three feet to the door, and twenty feet to the door. Indeed, during the workshop, Joe becomes most engaged when he is using spatial relationships to focus the play, and spacing out the set from a strict, naturalistic version to allow the symbolic tensions at the heart of the play to be seen more clearly.

Working backwards

On the fourth day, Joe wants to explore the play's final scene, in which Tom tells the audience that he left the apartment 'not long after' the debacle with Jim, the gentleman caller. In the play's final line, Tom asks his sister, who is illuminated in memory in a separate space onstage, to 'blow out her candles'. Joe cites the advice of one of his mentors, the Young Vic's artistic director, David Lan, who suggests that to understand a play, a director might start with the final scene, which is often 'the reason a play exists'. Joe's instinct is that whatever happened in St Louis must have been so long-lasting in its hold over Tom that he creates a play to make sense of it.

Joe first assumed that, in Tom's mind, the unforgivable sin was to leave, but the text tells you that in an evening of recollections, Tom does not replay the memory of him sneaking away. He only says 'a few days later, I left', which follows the centrepiece of the play, the scene between Laura and Jim, in which Laura attains happiness for a few moments, only to have it snatched away when Jim reveals that he is engaged to another woman.

Joe asks a group member to research what happened to Tennessee Williams's sister Rose, who is arguably the template for Laura. 'What does Laura lose when Jim leaves? What is her fate? Electroshock? Lobotomy?' The research tells us that Edwina, Tennessee's mother, committed Rose to an asylum when Rose was in her late twenties, following years of her strange behaviour. Rose received convulsive therapy and was eventually subjected to a lobotomy that left her incoherent for life.

A combination of the play's structure and the research leads Joe to believe that the play is not in fact the story of Tom leaving: it's the story of the night Tom's sister was damaged.

> It's everything that led up to that night, and why that night is so important. The worst thing Tom does is the evening with Jim. That evening is worse than his decision to leave the house. The decision to leave is, of course, massive, but the thing Tom cannot get over is his complicity in the evening that damaged Laura irreversibly; the night that broke her.

The group tracks backwards through the play to the end of the first half, to Tom smoking out on the fire escape and his mother asking that he find a gentleman caller for Laura. The script gives Tom the words to agree to the request after some bombardment from Amanda. Joe feels the scene is an offer made by Amanda and accepted by Tom, a deal done in return for a guilt-free escape from the flat. With Laura married, Tom would be freed from his burden of supporting her.

To examine the scene, Joe asks two members of the group to play Tom and Amanda. They sit on two of a closed circle of chairs that represents the apartment. They play the scene with the restriction that they must remain seated, but can shuffle around the chairs. The scene becomes a cat-and-mouse game with Amanda chasing Tom. The instinct is comedy: Amanda is a force of nature, and she wears his resistance until he acquiesces: anything so she will leave him alone to enjoy his cigarette.

The next exercise takes the scene in another direction. The chairs are removed except two, which are placed directly opposite each other, a few metres apart. The group members playing Tom and Amanda sit, facing each other, with no scripts in their hands. Two other people read the lines clearly and without emotion, which the pair repeat. The rule is that they must not break eye contact.

Subtext starts to seep from the words. In the gaps between waiting for the next line, the pair are given more time to think about the offer that is each line, and the sense develops that Tom comes to understand and consider what his mother is asking. Joe suggests that this scene might be thought of not only as a pact, but as Tom agreeing to something that he knows won't work, so that so he can say, 'I tried.' 'The pact is explicit,' Joe says. 'What's more interesting is that Tom suspects that what will happen next will damage Laura, but he does it anyway.' For the actor playing Tom to carry this information with him throughout the play is to affect every interaction he has with Laura.

Music

On the last day of the workshop, Mike Walker and Dario Marianelli, respectively the production's sound designer and composer, attend rehearsals to discuss music, which is an important part of any production of *The Glass Menagerie*.

Mike starts work by listing every sound and music cue in the script. He then divides the list into cues that might be recorded and cues that might be live. The recorded cues will be sourced mostly from sound archives; the live cues will be written by Dario. Tom, in the script, mentions music coming from a 'fiddle in the wings'. In this production, there will be two musicians visible in the gallery above the stage. One will play the piano, the other will play a percussion, including a glass harmonica, whose ethereal quality expresses the fantasy worlds in which the characters seek refuge, such as Laura's glass menagerie.

Today, Mike and Joe are to discuss the music that spills into the Wingfields' apartment from a nearby nightclub, the Paradise Dance Hall. The sound will be sourced from an archive, and to find an effective piece, Mike considers not only the era, but the smallest differences between musical genres and orchestration, such as the difference between the big-band sound of the 1940s and the smaller ensembles of the 1930s. Music with lyrics is ruled out for its tendency to compete with dialogue for the audience's attention. Similarly distracting are uptempo numbers, which can conflict with the tempo of a speaking voice, and pieces where the timbre of the lead instrument is similar to the human voice (particularly the reedy sound of clarinets).

Joe and Mike agree that whatever pieces they use should be recordings by the same artist to suggest the presence of a house band. This in turn sets boundaries on the type of ensemble that a nightclub could afford to hire, which would be a relatively small ensemble. They settle on recordings by the jazz quintet fronted by the trombonist Jack Teagarden.

Rehearsal ➡

Rehearsals for the production proper begin soon after the second workshop.

In casting the production, Joe casts the pivotal roles first. Jim is cast to contrast with Tom, for example, rather than vice versa. The cast comprises Leo Bill (Tom), Deborah Findlay (Amanda), Sinéad Matthews (Laura) and Kyle Soller (Jim).

Research

The company begins by looking together at the script, extracting information to help them start to build Tennessee Williams's St Louis, which is a vast, sprawling world populated by the ghosts of offstage characters, pregnant with history and full of unfamiliar references, from the Daughters of the American Revolution to Celotex; from Durkee's dressing to Famous-Barr. Working together, the company compiles lists of every person and place that the play mentions, and constructs timelines of the events that lead up to the action. They pin these to the walls of the rehearsal room alongside broader research into Tennessee Williams's life.

Most of this information will not pay off in present action; rather, it provides tangential clues that layer to create a world that might feel authentic and tangible. Sometimes, however, the research does have tangible results, such as the realisation that 'Blue Mountain', the period that Amanda loves to relive and relate, when she was young and desired by strings of gentleman callers, occurred in a shorter space of time than the company had assumed. 'We realised that Amanda is probably talking about a year of her life,' Joe reflects. 'That helps us understand how intense that period must have been, but it also makes more tragic the fact that she never moved on from it.'

The more Joe reads the play, the more it convinces him that it is about 'all the things that aren't written in it'. As a rule, Joe doesn't obsess about author's lives, but *The Glass Menagerie* contains too many parallels to Tennessee Williams's life to ignore. Tennessee's birth name was Tom and, like his namesake, he spent his early adulthood working in a shoe factory to support his mother and sister, and struggling to find the space to write creatively. Williams's memoir, published in 1975, detailed his sexual encounters as a young man in the back rows of the cinemas of St Louis, which cannot help but inform a director's reading of Tom's private life. 'Writers are often trying simultaneously to show something and conceal something,' Joe says:

> The parallels between a writer's life and the play don't necessarily add anything overt to the production – what can you say to the actor beyond pointing out the similarities? – but the detail might help you see what's already there. Research is about feeding the actors in the scenes. It can help an actor to know what happens before a scene, so knowing that Tennessee Williams went cruising in cinemas might help Leo [the actor playing Tom] to understand the night that Tom comes home from the cinema drunk. There is an extremity in Tom's life, which is almost hidden, although hinted at, in the play. Research tells us that Tennessee would burn himself out writing and suffered successive breakdowns, and that his sister's mental state was extremely fragile. That is where the information may be useful to the actor.

Building the apartment

As Joe explained, design is more than 'a set': it is the production itself. Without a final design, he doesn't have 'enough of a sense of the language of the production, certainly not enough to be able to translate it into a language that will help the actors move within that space'. To play the characters, the actors who play Amanda, Laura and Jim need to understand, for example, whether they are ghosts of Tom's memory who return to the toy box of memory between scenes, or actors Tom employs to re-enact scenes in his life.

When rehearsals begin, there is no final design, without which Joe says he 'doesn't know how to rehearse the play'. He reflects that the first days were 'difficult'.

As Joe and Jeremy refine the design, the company builds a 'real' version of the Wingfield apartment without reference to the Young Vic's auditorium or to concepts or themes or sight lines. The smallness of the apartment impresses itself, and the company begins to understand, physically, the particular hell of the cosmopolitan adult man who lives with his mother with barely a curtain between them, and of the mother and the daughter who long for a room of their own.

With the apartment built, Joe sets exercises to happen with that space. These are improvisations of events in the characters' pasts, such as a scene in which Amanda nurses Laura. 'Improvisation is about layering of a set of experiences,' Joe explains.

> Actors don't necessarily remember a specific improvisation onstage, but the company comes to share a rich psychological history and a series of emotional connections with each other, as one does in real life. I hope that, in some way, that informs the performance.

Improvisations can also be used as a more explicit tool for direction. For example, in the play's second scene,

216

Amanda learns that Laura has been concealing the fact that she dropped out of a college course that Amanda paid for her to attend. To direct Sinéad Matthews (Laura), Joe reminds her of an improvisation in which Amanda nursed Laura and asks that she remember how 'Laura's mother looked after her', which unlocks Laura's guilt and heightens her sense of being a burden.

A director's personal connection to the text

Part of the actor's job is to inhabit and present the conflicts within his character, Joe says. 'That is not always comfortable.' Part of directing, therefore, is to guide actors into emotional territory that they might rather avoid. Naturally, an actor – and indeed a director – will gravitate towards the aspects of a character with whom they share an affinity, or skip over an aspect that feels too close to home, or that they simply don't recognise. *The Glass Menagerie* asks its actors to consider such terrifying emotions as having abandoned someone you love, hating your family, and even addresses the all-consuming fear that one's life stalled many years ago.

'In a way, a summary of the director's job is to help actors go to the place they don't want to,' Joe says. He believes that a director's most important contribution to a production is to bring what he has experienced and felt in the real world into his direction of the play. He says that the 'most brilliant, but devastating' note he ever received from a peer was when he directed a workshop production of Chekhov's *Uncle Vanya* at the Young Vic.

> Someone who knew me well said, 'I know you, and I know that you know things about what that character is going through, and yet you haven't put it in the production. You haven't got the actor to inhabit and express those feelings.' The solution could be to set up an improvisation to find the missing emotional colour,

or it might be a note on the line, or it might come from the situation. Everything you do should be from the play and for the play, but if you don't bring *yourself* to the play, then what, really, are you doing? Directing is highly personal, yet completely collaborative, because the story is written by someone else and filtered through other people and completely dependent on them and governed by their work. We're sometimes told that having a particularly strong emotional reaction to something in a play could blind us, but as long as it's coupled to rigorous analysis... that's the point, isn't it? You *should* be obsessed with it. It works in a strange way: I wouldn't say that *The Glass Menagerie* is 'the story of my life' but I'm drawn to plays that focus on family, also sexuality. That covers pretty much all the plays I've ever directed. I've done two plays about mother–daughter relationships – I'm neither a mother nor a daughter, but you bring to it what you can and that's part of the job. A director should feel the emotion of the script himself and feed it back into the production, which should express some of the deepest, darkest, personal things about how you see your life and where you come from.

Directing the company

Directing, Joe says, is 'really about getting actors to move and explore ways of expressing thoughts and feelings'. He advises strongly against using the early rehearsals to fix exactly where the actors should move, or precisely how they should say their lines. Instead, the actors need to be given time, with the director's support, to explore the play and the space it's happening in, before the director focuses them on particular choices or interpretations:

> Your job early on is to ask the actors specific questions and set them practical tasks so that they start to find it for themselves. It's pointless to dictate a physical move or a way of thinking before an actor understands the part – why the character's moving, or why they feel the

way they do. If, on day one, you tell the actors exactly how to do it, then they're entitled to tell you to fuck off and give them some space. That said, the actors will probably do what you ask, but it'll be hollow and it'll go stale quickly.

This is not to say that Joe believes that directors should be afraid of telling people what to do. Far from it. 'Actors want leadership as much as they want facilitation of their own work,' he says, and if that sounds like a contradiction, perhaps it is. 'Directing is full of contradictions,' he says.

> Nothing about directing is simple, just as nothing elsewhere in life in simple. You wouldn't think that simply doing 'a', 'b' and 'c' would get you the job you want, or the girl you fancy, and you can't direct a play that way either. It appeals to think that there could be a way of conducting yourself or leading a process that could make it free from dilemmas or stress; that if you do 'a', 'b' and 'c,' everything will be fine but the truth is: it's hard, shit happens and you won't always know what you're doing. That is not to say that directing is random: you use technique and your conceptual understanding, for example, of dramatic action and psychology, but 'The Right Thing to Do' isn't always obvious in advance. Every day, a director makes judgements on a continuum between guiding and telling, instructing and suggesting, stepping in and stepping back. You have to judge the room moment by moment. Principles and craft are useful, but if they made the job easy, anyone could do it.

Starting a scene

Actions in life, as in theatre, are powered by detailed character histories, but also in the immediate past, which is to say what happened immediately before a scene. For example, the argument between Laura and Amanda over Laura's exit from business school is more interesting when the actors and the director consider that Amanda was on her way to be inducted into an exclusive social club, the Daughters of the American Revolution, when she heard the news.

Joe often finds it useful to improvise the moments immediately before a scene, to get the actors on their feet and interacting with each other and the space, so that the scene 'isn't being pulled from nowhere'. Rehearsing the scene in Act 2 in which Amanda makes last-minute alterations to Laura's dress ahead of Jim's arrival, Joe lists everything that needs to be done to prepare the flat, and asks Deborah Findlay (Amanda) to enlist Sinéad Matthew's (Laura's) help in doing so. He only asks that the actors prepare the environment, but as they fetch the bowls and cutlery and unveil Laura's dress from its box, their interactions take on the characters of Amanda and Laura, with Deborah starting to speak as Amanda, correcting Sinéad and leading the process. 'The exercise began as Deborah and Sinéad, but they became Amanda and Laura,' Joe says. 'When we ran the scene immediately afterwards, it was amazing.'

Finalising the design

Two weeks into rehearsal, the design solidifies. The space will appear untreated, as if the audience has walked into a theatre between productions. The stage is composed of exposed steeldeck. Costume rails and a 'backstage' area are set upstage. Two musicians wearing black will be visible above.

The space will be transformed from this naked aesthetic through some theatrical magic involving a red curtain and the contribution of light and sound.

The pre-set: everything exposed in working light. A world of steeldeck and theatre walkways represent the harsh reality of Depression-era St Louis. The curtain goes up and the set is transformed, made magical by light and music.

Every moment is a symphony

A principle of Joe's work is that no moment exists onstage without a reason. Back during the first workshop, the group staged the scene in which Amanda asks Tom to find a gentleman caller for Laura. The main action of the scene is her request and Tom's agreement. However, that doesn't happen for ten minutes. The accepted practice for writers is to start a scene as close as possible to its critical event; therefore, Joe reasons, the first ten minutes of the scene must be about something else, which triggers a new process of interrogating the text.

Similarly, the second act begins with Amanda setting the 'pretty trap' for Jim that is her daughter. Laura stands in the dress she will wear for dinner whilst Amanda makes last-minute alterations. The script asks that Laura 'moves slowly to [a] long mirror and stares solemnly at herself'. In this, Joe finds thirty whole seconds of wordless action – patterns of tension and release.

The stand-in for the mirror during the workshop is a flipchart on wheels. Joe places this at the other end of the set, so Amanda has to fetch it. A few seconds stretch into an eternity as Laura waits to see her reflection. Joe develops the tension of this moment, placing the mirror downstage and having Laura begin the scene facing upstage. In this version, when Laura turns to see herself, she turns downstage to the mirror, and the audience's response is synced with hers. A third version removes Amanda from the scene altogether, which gives Laura a rare moment, free from criticism, to enjoy her appearance. These three versions develop a single stage direction, and embody the principle that no moment onstage is merely connective tissue to the next big event.

Previews ➡

With the production reaching tech rehearsals, Joe feels, more than he has before, that he cannot tell whether the production works. 'Who has ever made a show without having a moment of thinking: "There's no way this is going to work"?' he says, but on this production he feels it acutely, partly because the play is so complex and partly because the technical elements, which arrive so late in the process, are so much part of the production:

> Every production element comes together in an absurdly short space of time – like two days – and you're sat in the auditorium thinking, 'Wow… okay… so this is what I wanted but perhaps not in a way I expected.' We had the expressionistic music and lighting in our heads from the start, but it's another thing entirely when you're in the theatre and it's in front of you.

The theatre director is forever battling a sense that the piece is incomplete. It is inherent in theatre that the creative elements of a production are intertwined. With film, by contrast, the picture is locked in the edit suite before a composer adds the music score. Joe reflects that there is no 'picture-lock' in theatre, which is 'never finished' and 'if it is, it is finished only in such a way that it has to be remade the next day by the actors. This is good and bad, pleasurable and painful, unfortunate and fortunate,' he says.

When he is battling the feeling of incompletion, Joe channels 'the best advice anyone ever gave him', which is to trust the process. Even in rehearsal, a director may struggle to accept that the piece is not ready for an audience. 'Particularly young directors want the production to be ready straightaway,' he says.

> I know I did. But learning to deal with that sense of unreadiness is important. The more I work, the better I get at bringing a production to boil at the right time

> which, at least for starters, is press night. You have to hold
> your nerve and trust that you will get there in the end.

It is, he warns, easy to be tricked into thinking that the deadline for the work being 'ready' is the first run in the rehearsal room, which usually happens at the end of the fourth week of rehearsals. Thinking that the production is developing too slowly, the director might start pushing, trying to 'fix' and starting to dictate instead of continuing the process of slowly heating the production and adding layers.

Now, when he starts work on a production, Joe counts the number of days backwards from press night and marks the halfway point in the process wherever it falls:

> If you're lucky enough to have five weeks of rehearsal
> and six previews, as you do at the Young Vic, then you
> calculate that there are five weeks in the rehearsal room,
> and one to tech and start performances, so press night is
> halfway through week seven. That means the halfway
> point in the process is halfway into week four. Usually in
> week four, you're panicking that you only have six days
> left in the rehearsal room. That is when you need to
> stand back and remember how far you've travelled from
> day one, and that you have exactly that time again. So
> trust the process and think about where the halfway
> point is, because it's almost always a relief to work it out.

Much of the early work of previews is hitting 'the big conceptual stuff' that gets the story working, Joe says. In this case, that means integrating the technical elements of the performances. The production team spends days re-teching lighting and changing music cues to help connect Tom explicitly to the play's theatrical language.

The first preview begins with the curtain down, obscuring the playing space. Leo Bill's Tom performs the opening monologue, in which he explains how the play will work, from the side of the stage. Then the curtain raises and Tom walks into the scene, which is the Wing-field family at breakfast. During the interval, Joe is standing on the street, talking to the director Rufus Norris, an associate of the theatre. Rufus tells him, 'politely and articulately', that the production hasn't yet clarified that the reality of the play is shaped by Tom's subjectivity; it's not clear that Tom is running the show and that the audience is somehow in his head. 'The best notes don't necessarily give you the solution,' Joe says, 'but they articulate for you the problem.' That evening, he raises Rufus's point with the creative team. The stakes are high. The company is tired and stressed, and doesn't have many previews left. 'It's one thing to change a production element,' Joe says. 'It would be destabilising to change something, then change it back.'

Jeremy Herbert arrives at rehearsal the next morning with a suggestion: when the audience enters, the curtain could be down. The entire theatre would be completely exposed. Leo could enter in full house light and gesture for the musicians to play. The curtain could rise, reveal-ing Amanda and Laura seated for breakfast as though a magician has waved a handkerchief over the set.

This solution foreshadows the scene in which Tom returns late at night from a magic show and demon-strates for Laura one of the tricks he saw, in which the magician waves a 'magic scarf' over a canary cage which is transformed into a bowl of goldfish. Back in the workshops, Joe was fascinated by the image and had wondered aloud whether the 'magic aspect' of the play should be presented, and how. The workshop had moved on, and the idea hadn't found a specific expres-sion, until now. 'It goes to show that you can have all the elements, but you don't always know how to employ them until the last minute,' Joe says.

The Director's Role ➡

The Glass Menagerie was a critical hit, the reviewer from the *Daily Telegraph* going so far as to hail a 'deeply felt, beautifully judged production of a masterpiece', although for balance the reviewer in the *Stage* felt that the production took an 'intensely mannered approach' that 'threatened to overburden the play with even more symbolic weight than it already carries'.

The Young Vic extended the run to meet the demand for tickets.

When we meet to reconstruct the production, Joe reflects that the experience was 'incredibly important' in his development, as the material reached beyond the naturalism that dominates so much of British theatre, towards an expressionistic aesthetic. One of the biggest influences in Joe's career has been German theatre. As an emerging director, Joe spent ten days watching productions at Theatertreffen, a theatre festival in Berlin, where he saw productions of new British plays including *A Number* by Caryl Churchill, although it was a production of *Othello* directed by Stefan Pucher that 'blew [his] mind'.

Early in researching *The Glass Menagerie*, Joe and Jeremy flew to Berlin to watch a production of the play at the Maxim Gorki Theater, *Das Glasmenagerie*. The production was modern-dress, used actors of broadly similar ages and featured a sequence in which Laura swims through a wash of blue light, wearing a perspex unicorn's head.

American English is close enough to British English that American plays are usually performed in their original context, without consideration for historical and cultural differences, which in a play like *The Glass*

Menagerie are considerable. Early in the first workshop, Joe asked the group to imagine that they were mounting a production of *The Glass Menagerie* in another language, without the cosy allure of the Deep South and the idiosyncrasies of its language. He asked the group to imagine a production of the play that took nothing for granted. 'What aspects of Tennessee Williams's world would you want the audience to experience most acutely?' he asked.

In this, Joe brings something of Berlin back to the UK, combining a love of the visceral with the rigorous text analysis and respect for the writer that you would expect from a British director who trained at the Royal Court. The synthesis creates a production that the reviewer from the *Independent* considered 'as conceptually fresh as it is emotionally devastating', the latter being more of a concern to many Brits than the former.

'At least fifty per cent of directing is done before you step into the rehearsal room,' Joe says.

> By the time you step into rehearsals, you have designed and cast the production, and contained within that is an expression of the concept and vision for the production. Conceiving a production is half of directing, and that's an important point.

Between the second workshop and rehearsals for the production proper, I mentioned something of this to an acquaintance who had rolled her eyes and said that workshops were a symptom of 'self-indulgent', subsidised theatres, with their overlong, taxpayer-funded rehearsal processes. She reasoned that, after fifty years of productions of the play and critical evaluation, there could be nothing about the play that we didn't already know.

But through two workshops, Joe and Jeremy took nothing for granted about the text. The endeavour to me recalls the mathematician and philosopher Bertrand Russell, who went back to basics to prove that one plus one equals two. To do so is to follow every lead: it is to tear up the design when it becomes 'too comfortable' during a workshop and insist that everyone starts again; it is in Jeremy giving himself the freedom to question out loud whether the production even needs a literal fire escape in its design.

An exhilarating production, it would appear, starts with no defaults.

The Wingfields at dinner – The Glass Menagerie *workshop*

The Wingfields at dinner – The Glass Menagerie *in production*

OperaUpClose

Don Giovanni

by Wolfgang Amadeus Mozart
(music) and Lorenzo Da Ponte
(libretto)

Soho Theatre

Mission Statement

OperaUpClose was founded in October 2009 by Adam Spreadbury-Maher, Ben Cooper and Robin Norton-Hale for the experiment of producing *La Bohème* at the Cock Tavern Theatre, a thirty-five-seat venue above a pub in Kilburn.

In October 2010, OperaUpClose became the resident company at the King's Head Theatre, relaunching the venue as 'an off-West End alternative to the Royal Opera House and the English National Opera'.

Christina Gill (Elvira) and Richard Immerglück (Alexander)

Don Giovanni
by Wolfgang Amadeus Mozart (music) and
Lorenzo Da Ponte (libretto)

Opened at Soho Theatre, London, on 11 August 2011

Creative
Director **Robin Norton-Hale**
Musical Director **Emily Leather**
Designer **Cherry Truluck**
Live Electronic Score **Harry Blake**
Lighting Designer **Phil Hewitt**

Cast
Johnny **Marc Callahan, Paul Carey Jones,
  Maciek O'Shea**
Alexander **Dickon Gough, Richard Immerglück,
  Tom Stoddart**
Anna **Fleur de Bray, Claire Egan, Elinor Jane Moran**
Elvira **Rosalind Coad, Christina Gill,
  Joanna Marie Skillet**
Zerlina **Stephanie Bodsworth, Emily-Jane Thomas**
Nathaniel **Marcin Gesla, Miles Horner**
Octavius **Robin Bailey, Anthony Flaum**
Commendatore **Gerard Delrez, Martin Nelson**
Chorus **Siân Cameron, Spiro Fernando, Peter Horton,
  Edward Lee , Rebecca Shanks, Louisa Tee**

Don Giovanni, the Opera →

'Don Giovanni is a psychopath,' says Robin Norton-Hale, the director of a new production of Mozart's morality tale, named after its foremost sinner: an aristocrat who lies and philanders his way through life, rejecting successive opportunities to mend his ways until the universe itself dispatches supernatural forces that drag him to Hell.

A month before performances begin at Soho Theatre, the company is road-testing the libretto, which Robin has adapted from the eighteenth-century Italian into English. As she listens to the performers, she marks in pencil where the scansion lifts an odd word in a phrase ('How do you think he *got* in?') or splits one thought across two phrases ('I know that/I could never replace him').

Don Giovanni is Robin's third production for Opera-UpClose after its inaugural production, *La Bohème*, which relocated the story to contemporary London, and a version of *The Barber of Seville* that transported the story to the England of Jane Austen. Her version of *Don Giovanni* is more freely translated than either: not only does it anglicise the locations and characters' names, but it redraws some of the relationships and plot points, developing a relatively straightforward morality tale (albeit with comic elements) into something else.

A wealthy nobleman in the original, Robin's Don Giovanni – Johnny – is a city trader in the months leading up to the global financial crisis of 2008. Johnny believes that the good times will last for ever and has the wealth to indulge every physical whim. Robin says that a challenge in staging the piece is that 'it asks the audience to spend two hours in the company of somebody they will hate, yet almost will forward'.

Don Giovanni's servant Leporello becomes Johnny's intern Alexander; Masetto, whose wife Johnny promises to steal, becomes the kind of Shoreditch hipster whose identity exists primarily in its opposition to 'braying men in pinstripe suits'; and the lady in question, Elvira, is given the nagging doubt that she married beneath herself.

Robin removes a convention of drama of the period, that characters can disguise their identities by wearing masks. 'Masks bug me,' she says, reflecting that a woman who sleeps with a man will know the shape of his face, his smell, the tone of his voice. Moreover, the illusion is harder to accept for an audience in an intimate playing space.

Fringe Opera ➡

That opera is widely considered ossified is attested by the incredible news coverage that the company's first production, *La Bohème*, received, having staged the production in a pub and drawn the characters as recognisably modern: the penniless blogger, the dodgy landlord, the Eastern European cleaner making her way in an unfamiliar city.

The stereotype of the opera aficionado is of a grey-haired couple, traditionally educated and exacting in their taste. Whilst it is true that many opera companies have recently awoken to the importance of expanding their subscriber base through outreach programmes and more accessible productions, it is also true that many opera fans like things 'just so'. Literate in a work's performance history and versed in the minute variations between recordings, some fans of opera feel particularly entitled to comment on scenes or arias that aren't, in their judgement, presented 'properly'.

Robin does not believe the production of *La Bohème* was so 'revolutionary' as the media led people to believe. 'As someone who goes to the theatre a lot, I felt I was just doing a modernised version of a famous opera in a fringe venue,' she says.

> Incidentally, I don't believe that all operas performed today need to be updated or set in modern times. But no one says that an hour-long version of *Hamlet* 'isn't Shakespeare'. You can even switch the genders of characters and no one blinks, but people kept wanting to say how daring our production was when all I did was update the libretto and set the story in Kilburn. I didn't changed a note except for a cut in Act 2 because we couldn't have children in the cast.

OperaUpClose's *La Bohème* was intended as an exercise, a low-stakes way to see whether 'opera singers would be prepared to work in a gritty, fringe environment', and then if anyone would even want to see a fringe opera. But as the ground swelled, Robin realised that she was at the epicentre of something bigger than anyone in the company, which was at the time little more than a name on a computer spreadsheet, had anticipated. 'We talk about the company as if we had some great plan,' she says. 'Of course, that wasn't the case at first. We had no idea if it would work. We certainly never thought that less than two years later, we would be producing full-time.'

The Score ⟹

The adaptor of a classic play or a Broadway musical who reduces the physical size of a production or orchestra may be embraced for having distilled the work to its 'essence'. But the orchestration of an opera, often created by the composer, is more likely to be considered part of the score rather than an expansion of it – indeed, many classical composers will tell you that this 'wholeness of vision' is one component of the difference between a composer and a mere 'songwriter'. To present an opera with a band that is too small, they fear, is not merely to remove the unnecessary adjectives from its sentence, but to have bowdlerised it entirely.

OperaUpClose's first productions were accompanied by piano only, an instrument that, whilst it has a expressive texture of its own, often suggests, through its association with fringe theatre, the reduced; the anaemic. Soon, Robin and her co-artistic director, Adam Spreadbury-Maher, committed the company to finding 'something more'.

But how to augment the score without the budget or space to accommodate an orchestra? The company's first experiments in rearrangement were with its productions of Puccini's *Madam Butterfly* and Leoncavallo's *Pagliacci*, which expanded the piano score for a trio and quartet, respectively, playing a version of the original orchestration. The next stage, taken with Mark Ravenhill's adaptation of *The Coronation of Poppea*, was to adapt the score more freely, in this case with Alex Silverman filtering Monteverdi's score through the language of jazz.

With *Don Giovanni*, OperaUpClose is exploring a different palette: electronic music. The conversation began with the realisation that, even if the production could afford a string section, the players would need to be 'astonishing'. 'Even then, we wouldn't be able to afford enough of them,' Robin says. The company decided to go in the opposite direction. Instead of reducing Mozart's orchestration, they would commit to finding a way to indicate the score's texture without using any of the original instruments.

To develop the score, Robin recruited Harry Blake, a classically trained composer with experience of electronic music. 'Harry understands Mozart,' she says. 'He is unafraid of tearing up the score because he has the classical grounding to do so with respect.' Harry attends the singthrough. He pulls up a table next to the beautiful Steinway grand piano played by the production's musical director, Emily Leather, and sets up a laptop, into which he plugs a small, plastic keyboard.

Recorded music has long been used in live theatre to reinforce a smaller live band. Productions of musicals, for example, often tour with recordings of short sections of music that will bolster the live band at moments of high drama and musicality. The idea with *Don Giovanni* is that recorded sound will not only reinforce the live sound, but deconstruct and counterpoint it, providing a different texture altogether.

Rehearsals →

A 'backwards' process

Directing text-based theatre versus opera can feel 'as different as directing film and theatre,' says Adam Spreadbury-Maher, the co-artistic director of OperaUpClose, who trained as an opera singer, but has since worked mostly as a director of text-based theatre. He discovered this to his cost when he directed *Madam*

Butterfly for the company, an experience that was, he says, the 'most stressful and counter-intuitive' of his career so far.

Adam recalls that acting lessons comprised a small part of his training as an opera singer, and were regarded by some of the students as 'that hour of the week when some crazy hippy makes us move our bodies'. Indeed, there is a perception among some theatremakers that opera is a director's medium, and consists of singers singing beautifully, but who are bussed around the stage on tracks in productions designed to within an inch of their lives by directors. Perhaps this notion is the result of some combination of opera's focus on the voice, a by-product of the 'signature productions' that larger opera companies unpack each year to tour, and instances of opera stars playing 'their' Don Giovanni in five or six productions, and even being flown to large opera houses last-minute to cover an injured singer.

If that singer, or an audience member who wants to see him, exists, it is not someone that Robin wants to entertain. 'We want the actors onstage to connect with each other,' she says, and argues that a new generation of opera singer is rising fast.

> My experience has been that the director needs to come to rehearsal with a clear idea of who the characters are and why they act as they do because, yes, some opera singers simply refuse *not* to be prescribed to. But on the other hand, because they are more likely to be able to sit in rehearsal and talk about that *other* production of *La Bohème* that they were in, some performers come to rehearsal wanting to differentiate their character from the ones they've seen before. When I find performers who want to do that and collaborate, I make sure we work together.

Singthrough

The initial singthrough brings the company together to hear the score in Robin's new English-language version, which must wrap new words around a score known well to those who will sing it. The experience can be profoundly anxious for the adaptor. 'English spoken sounds so different to English sung,' Robin says. 'Lines that work on the page often sound wrong when sung, and vice versa.'

The performers have many questions about the version. The repertoire of commonly performed operas is relatively small and so, whilst actors in 'straight theatre' often audition for plays they were not inclined to read until they saw the casting notice, 'very few bass-baritones, for example, will have trained and not thought about how they will play, for example, Leporello some day,' Robin observes.

OperaUpClose won an Olivier Award for Puccini's *La Bohème*, but that is the past. A director can refer neither cast nor audience to her last success: all that matters is the production before her, which fights for a life of its own.

Opera is hard going on the voice (infamously so), and whilst the performance run of a large-scale opera might be ten performances spaced across a few weeks or months, OperaUpClose will perform *Don Giovanni* eight times a week. Therefore, many of the roles will be shared by two or three performers, performing each night in different combinations. An actor arrives late. He has not met the other actors with whom he will share his role, and when he asks where they are sitting, I resist the nerve to suggest he looks at the huddles of twos and threes and decides which of them looks most like him.

Like most companies, OperaUpClose is unfunded. Opera is expensive to produce, especially with three sets of actors on Equity rates. And so money hangs over the discussion, as it does in rehearsal rooms the world over. Robin half-jokes that the gin bottles, which are to be a feature of the set design, will be 'whichever brand might sponsor us', and Cherry Truluck, the designer, explains that as many costumes as possible will be borrowed or adapted from donations, although this turns out to be unnecessary.

Robin asks the performers to start thinking of any witty anecdotes they might have stored in their memories, as a broadsheet journalist is to visit rehearsals next week to write a preview feature, and this is 'a chance to sell tickets'.

The piano

The work of rehearsal begins at the piano. Emily Leather, the music director, refreshes the score with the performers, who focus at first so intently on the score in their hands that everything else in the room seems to melt away. Trained opera singers are, as a group, technically adept: they can read music (many adept musicians can't) and they have absolute control over their instrument, the voice. To paraphrase or speak-sing would be unthinkable, and the score is to be respected down to the last semi-quaver. As Emily takes the cast through the same, complex section of music for the third time, Robin observes that some opera directors choose to skip the first week of rehearsal altogether. 'Most opera performers want to get the notes right,' she says. 'They won't feel free to create characters until they are secure in the notes and confident that they're not making "a horrible sound".'

With this confidence, the singing can become 'almost incidental,' she adds. 'If the audience forgets that they are watching people singing, then we have removed one of the layers of artificiality that opera can struggle with.'

Sharing roles

The company starts as a unit, with an actor for each role present to discuss the scenes. One set rehearses in front of their counterparts, who offer contributions from their chairs. Sporadically, the teams swap over. The system means that there could be up to twenty people in the rehearsal room at any time.

Later, rehearsals will split into a sort of 'time-share' system, with Robin's assistant relaying notes to the other casts. Over time, some elements of the performances converge. Robin explains that, with three casts, some blocking must be set, if only so the performers can work in different combinations and feel safe. However, she finds that she adapts her process more than she might were there only one set of actors to work with. 'Really, it's three different processes,' she says. Some performers are very 'intellectual' – they might want to discuss a short section of text for forty-five minutes – whereas some find the character through movement. And some performers ask for blocking, which some directors consider to be frightfully old-fashioned. Robin is relaxed on the point. 'A company of actors is always a mixed bag,' she says.

> And we have that times three. Besides, for some actors, telling them to 'enter upstage-left then walk down on this or that line' will free them from worrying to create. And what each actor does whilst they're entering upstage-left, or walking downstage on the line might be completely different. So it's only restrictive if you let it.

Opera, up close

In a smaller playing space, an actor needn't produce a big sound or 'act by semaphore,' as they might in a large opera house. Rather, they can explore the depth and breadth of their voices, safe in the knowledge that the audience will hear every note. But as opera training tends to prepare performers for auditoriums that hold thousands, the challenge of performing in an intimate space can be destabilising.

Part of Robin's job is managing that transition. Some singers instinctively resist the assurance that they can move around the stage naturalistically and even turn their backs to the audience if they wish. They can act as if there is no audience at all. 'It's not as simple as doing "the same thing but smaller",' Robin says. 'The direction of their eyes or a flicker of their mouths can be read and take on meaning.' This imperative affects the text itself. The relationship between Johnny and Alexander, for example, which is reconfigured in the text from master–servant to boss–intern, assumes a 'matey' quality that is communicated in small interactions and glances that would be lost on a larger stage.

Ways of Seeing ➡️

With *Don Giovanni* in rehearsal, I watch another production of the piece, this time at the Glyndebourne Festival, in a production by the director Jonathan Kent. To get to Glyndebourne from London, you take a train from Victoria to Lewes followed by a dedicated coach. In the past year alone, I have attended a theatre performance that took place in total darkness, a performance in a moving car, a series of one-on-one 'encounters', and have been hauled on to the stage to improvise with a company in front of five hundred people. But as I sit on a coach, wearing a suit and surrounded by similarly dressed people, most of whom are very old and very white and have similar accents, I feel more uncomfortable than I ever have going to the theatre. My long-suffering partner, beautiful in her dress, squeezes my hand and begs me to have fun. These tickets, she says, were not easy to get hold of.

The grounds of Glyndebourne are maintained with military precision. For some who come here, the thought that goes into every aspect of the experience is the festival's unique appeal. Before the performance, I thumb through the programme, past adverts for wealth-management companies, country fashion and high-end hi-fi equipment. I look up at the stage from a £70 seat with a restricted view. Outside there are tea rooms, a croquet lawn and restaurants where the wine list tops at £450 a bottle. The door to the men's toilet is marked with a diagram of a man wearing a bow tie.

As the house lights dim, I feel my body tightening. I tell myself: 'This will not be for me.'

The production is breathtaking. It is moving, sad, funny, and theatrically and dramaturgically maverick. The score, played by the Orchestra of the Age of Enlightenment, levitates. This *is* visceral, albeit a different kind of visceral: visceral in that every sense is pricked, filled but not bombarded.

The first act climaxes with Don Giovanni eluding his pursuers. The curtain comes down and we walk back into the daylight. I am immediately embarrassed by my prejudice, and I am about to apologise to my partner, who has put up with me all day, when an octogenarian couple sit down next to us. They open a bottle of champagne and a box of strawberries and they start to discuss how 'exceptionally fine' and 'refreshingly civilised' they are finding the performance. I resist the urge to lean towards them. 'What part of the performance are you finding civilised? Is it the evocation of Hell or just the rape?'

A few weeks later, I am at Soho Theatre, watching the production by OperaUpClose. I am wearing jeans and a T-shirt, and holding a glass of beer. The audience's response to the performance, which comes in at a speedy two hours, is visceral in an entirely different way. Unlike the producers of Glyndebourne, OperaUpClose lacks the hard cash to back up its ambition. And so it approaches the material from a different angle, bringing *opera up close*, literally and metaphorically, with different theatrical modes.

Some of the reviews of *Don Giovanni* take issue with the freedom of Robin's adaptation, and with the 'thinned' orchestration. Robin accepts that the production does not present 'exactly what Mozart wrote', but counters that nor do many productions in larger houses. She points out that Mozart's operas are often performed in nineteenth-century opera houses, which differ vastly in acoustics from the theatres of Mozart's day, with augmented orchestras playing modern instruments, rather than the instruments of the period. 'I think there's room for the opera houses *and* us,' she says. 'We don't want to present "toned-down" versions of operas. We want to present something else entirely and combat the notion that opera is an untouchable form.'

A self-taught musician, Robin's father introduced her to opera when she was nine years old. They sat in the cheap seats at the English National Opera where performances are sung in English. 'I never associated opera with being posh,' she says. 'A trip to the opera was no different to a trip to see any other kind of theatre.'

I ask how I should refer to the company before I start to write this chapter. Should I refer to 'actors', 'singers' or 'performers'? In the traditional language of opera, a role is 'sung' rather than 'acted' or 'performed', which has connotations of acting from the lungs up, rather than *embodying* the part. 'Call them performers,' Robin says. 'That's what we're trying to work towards as a company.'

The test of OperaUpClose will be whether the media stops referring to fringe opera as a gateway drug towards 'serious' or 'proper' opera, and instead engage with the work on its own merits, as a complete experience. But, for now, fringe opera is an idea that has struck a chord with the popular imagination. Like all new art movements, it might help an audience see better, even if it's to see what was always there.

Action Hero

Frontman

Fierce Festival

Mission Statement

'Action Hero make live art and performance that uses audiences as collaborators and co-conspirators. We are interested in creating work that links audiences and unifies them as part of the live event, building a temporary community. Our process has been defined by necessity: our work often has a sense of the epic, even though it is played out through a lo-fi, DIY approach. Whilst exploring the epic, we create performance that is intimate, distinctive and invigorating.

We have been making performances as Action Hero since 2005. We are associate artists of Inbetween Time Productions and Forest Fringe, and we live and work in Bristol where we are members of Residence, a community of theatremakers who share space, resources, knowledge and opportunities in an old record shop.'

Action Hero

Gemma Paintin (The Frontman)

Frontman

Opened at Circomedia, Bristol, on 4 December 2010.

Action Hero is
Gemma Paintin and **James Stenhouse**

Frontman was co-commissioned by Inbetween Time Productions and Fierce Festival 2011. UK tour supported by Arts Council England. Supported by Forest Fringe and Residence.

An Unintentional Trilogy ➡

Action Hero announced itself with *A Western*, a performance for bars. The company, a collaboration between Gemma Paintin and James Stenhouse, were interested in Westerns, that staple of Americana, but lacking the practical experience to make a film (the genre's traditional medium) and uninterested in conventional plays with scripts and hired actors, they decided to make something else entirely.

The result was a performance that couldn't happen without the 'beautiful tool' of shared imagination, as the company arrived in each bar and, with the audience's imagination and complicity, willed the existence of the lawless West.

The lessons of *A Western* shaped Action Hero's core values. Not only did they find that each new performance space altered the production fundamentally, but the audience seemed more willing to engage with the performance the less the venue resembled a traditional theatre space.

A second show, *Watch Me Fall*, explored the psychology of the daredevil stuntman who risks death for a few moments of transcendence, and of his audience, which makes him a receptacle for its secret maverick desires. At its climax, the performance recreated Evel Knievel's infamous jump at Caesars Palace, a casino in Las Vegas.

Knievel crashed his motorbike and his injuries put him in a coma for a month.

Frontman forms the third part of an 'unintentional trilogy' about icons and masculinity. 'Cowboys and stuntmen are frontmen in a sense,' Gemma says. Just as *A Western* and *Watch Me Fall* asked the audience to help create the Wild West and Las Vegas, *Frontman* engages with the format of a rock concert. 'It's interesting to ask what you can borrow from live performances that isn't theatre.'

There are two strands to the idea. There is a fascination with rock 'n' roll's iconic frontmen (and a few women), the icons whose music and performance culture defined eras and persists to this day. There is Elvis Presley, Iggy Pop, Kurt Cobain, Dolly Parton.

The second strand embraces the dissonance and atonality of underground scenes, from punk to live-art bands like Skinny Puppy. Whilst their fascination with the world of live music comes from their experience of attending gigs and considering how the relationship between the performers and the crowds tends to work, neither James nor Gemma have played in bands. Nor are they musicians, and so they come to this world as outsiders. 'There is an element of fear for us here,' James says. 'That's interesting to us.'

Gathering →

'There is no formula to how we work,' Gemma says. 'We haven't been together as a company for long, so we can't go into a room and, y'know, *bash, bash, bash!*'

An Action Hero production begins without a text. It has a long incubation period and finds its meaning through rehearsal. From the first seed to the finished show, *Frontman* will take eighteen months to develop, which is time fitted around other projects, mostly touring *Watch Me Fall*. Gemma estimates that she and James will have spent fifteen weeks on the project in total.

First, Gemma and James marinade themselves in primary sources. They listen to albums, watch hours of concert footage and read interviews and history books, which they convert to fuel for improvisation, in transcripts, articles and pictures drawn in school exercise books, stuck on the walls of the rehearsal room.

Early in the process, two images take centre stage. There is Elvis Presley as he appears in the 1968 TV movie *Elvis* (commonly known as the *'68 Comeback Special*), in which the star plays his first concert in seven years. He plays from a small stage, surrounded on all sides by an invited audience and he stops and starts songs, and banters with his fans. Gemma and James are interested in the high stakes of a singer who is aware of his legacy and eager to reinvent himself. This idea of the comeback special will become integral to the performance.

They also become interested in frontmen who sabotage their own work, or whose work begins to collapse in on itself through depression or after their lyrics are ripped from context, and reduced to aphorisms pasted on T-shirts. At the centre is Richey Edwards, the guitarist and chief lyricist of Manic Street Preachers, missing since 1995 and declared dead in 2008, who carved '4 Real' into his arm with a razor blade in front of a journalist who suggested that he might not mean everything he said.

Having filled two exercise books with notes and sketches, Gemma and James hold back 'as long as we can' before they start making the show. James explains:

If you were to count the hours, we probably spend more time drinking cups of tea and talking than making things in the rehearsal room. The rehearsal process is snipping and mashing and squashing all that mince into a kebab. We like to bank ideas, backing ourselves further against the wall until we have no choice but to jump on to the stage.

The Chelsea Theatre ➡

I meet the company at the end of the gathering stage, after months of discussion broken up by its committment to tour *Watch Me Fall*.

So far, there has been an eight-minute showing in Bristol, which found the company experimenting with 'extreme noise'. James says of the showing that it was 'rough and, in places, terrible. It was also very helpful.'

The next stage is a two-day workshop at the Chelsea Theatre, a live-art venue in West London.

James and Gemma ferry boxes of props and materials from the office to the rehearsal room, which is a converted schoolroom with a linoleum floor, a pull-down blackboard and lighting courtesy of two strip lights (two out of four work).

The props are instruments. There are two Buddha Machines, hand-held musical players that come loaded with nine ambient drones. These are plugged, via a distortion stomp-box, into a guitar amp. There is also a tambourine, a hand-held microphone and a laptop with a fully stocked iTunes library.

Gemma and James arrive with ideas for how the performance might be structured, and how they might start 'slotting bits of content together'. They begin by setting tasks to structure the rehearsal day and help fight the tyranny of the blank page. James lists a series of 'what ifs' on flipchart paper, and sticks them to the wall:

- What if the audience is split in two?
- What if the piece is composed of 'tracks'?
- What if there is a bar in the room?

They develop the material through improvisation. The scenario is a comeback gig. One of the performers will be a singer, and the performance will be a gig that is 'poised on the edge of catastrophe'. They decide to work on a slow song from the gig; the song that means something personal to the singer, but that the crowd don't want to hear; the weak track of the album, perhaps, or just the unwelcome moment of sincerity in an evening of greatest hits or uptempo tracks.

They agree ground rules:

- To use every object onstage at least once.
- Not to use any tech elements.
- To avoid replicating anything they've done so far.

First, Gemma will play the frontman and James will adopt the role of director, such as it is. James sets an environment for Gemma to work in. He hands her pieces of text that he would like her to speak, and chooses music for her to respond to. She improvises based on fragments of text, which are interviews with famous frontmen. She channels the ghosts of Elvis, Johnny Cash and Sid Vicious. She sings and berates the crowd for any number of perceived slights to her art.

James coaches from the side. 'We don't necessarily know what we're looking for,' he says afterwards. Indeed, the process resembles a chemistry experiment, adding different concentrations of elements to the scene, then reducing or boiling off some of the intensity whilst pouring in more of something else. When Gemma becomes blocked, James offers an assist, handing her a new piece of text or instructing her to repeat a theme or change subject. The skill lies in making an offer before the intensity of a moment has passed. When Gemma has had enough, they swap roles, as yet unsure who will do what in the final production. Each trusts the other's judgement to refine and guide their play. Often they disagree. Occasionally they bicker. They are a team whose strengths balance each other out.

The following day, they improvise together and for almost an hour, they play music, speak, compete and dance, sometimes together, sometimes apart, and sometimes as a challenge to each other. This is not work for an audience: at least half is impenetrable. But sporadically, something clicks, usually an emotional beat or a visually arresting image, such as when James ties the microphone cord around his neck like a noose, or Gemma finds herself overwhelmed by sound, light and the audience's affection. We have seen these images before, in concerts and in rock mythology. Here they achieve abstraction: the Platonic form of the frontman.

The improvisation ends with a shared look and immediately they start to reconstruct the improvisation on paper. Still panting for breath, Gemma writes a heading, 'Anything You Can Remember', and they list any images or moments that left an impression, good or bad.

Residence ➡

Fundamental questions about the production remain in flux much later than many companies might be comfortable with. Following the sessions at the Chelsea Theatre, Gemma and James are still unsure of the type of gig they want to recreate (stadium extravaganza or club), what role the audience will assume, and whether the ending should be 'a downer or an upper'. In the months that pass before I catch up with Gemma and James, they have 'a bit of a meltdown' as they experience the painful realisation that they aren't making the show they want to make.

'We kept banking ideas,' Gemma recalls. 'We had twenty pieces of A3 paper on the wall; all these moments with no transitions between. We couldn't see the wood for the trees and we were going round in circles, not addressing the big questions and not committing.'

A work-in-progress showing at the Edinburgh Fringe is deemed a failure. The audience is fundamental to Action Hero's work, and James and Gemma believe that they lost sight of that connection, instead barraging the audience with 'weird, aggressive things, unframed by context'. 'It needs to be beautiful and magnificent,' Gemma says. 'We haven't made it.' James corrects her. 'We haven't made it *yet*.'

In times of uncertainty, theatremakers turn to peers, mentors and friends who can help them refocus and who have no agenda beyond being helpful. Action Hero's base is a converted record shop in Bristol which they share with a number of other artists and companies who make theatre, performance and live art. More than a space, Residence is a community of theatremakers; a place to hang out, support and advise, share and celebrate. Whilst other makers toil in bedrooms and expensive rehearsal spaces, creating alone and engendering rivalry, the founders of Residence arranged with the council to take on a building, empty for six years, and repaint it, reconnect the gas and electricity, and call it home.

Occasionally, Gemma and James will share sketches of their work with the other companies at Residence. The process of receiving these notes is the closest they get to having a traditional director. 'Their questions help us develop the piece further,' James says. 'It could be: "Why are you doing that?" or "Do you realise this bit probably doesn't read as you intended?" or "Why don't you put this bit next?" or practical things like: "I can't hear you at that point."'

With the help of their peers, the project finds its focus. 'We wanted this show to push us,' Gemma says.

> It's definitely done that. We also realised that we needed to recognise our fear of the subject material, and of the fact that this is the first time we've had venues calling us instead of the other way around. It's amazing how emotional factors can affect a process, and you have to devise strategies to handle difficult situations instead of ignoring them.

I next see the company at Residence, six months after the Chelsea Theatre and less than a week before the show premieres at the Inbetween Time Festival at Circomedia, a 'big, old church' on Portland Square.

In a small rehearsal room on the ground floor, they are wired for sound. In place of the Buddha Machines and the iTunes library, there is now an analogue synthesiser, a bank of knobs and junction of wires that create purrs and growls at ear-splitting volume.

There is renewed focus in the rehearsal room. Having spent over a year sharpening the axe, it is time to fell the tree. The show is getting leaner as the pair order the material, cutting instances of repetition or 'anything that isn't taking us somewhere new', finding the peaks in the tension and working on the transitions between sections. They agree that tomorrow is the last day to change anything structural: 'We'll keep changing things if we're not tough with ourselves.' Wednesday to Saturday, they will fine-tune the performance and repeat.

The performance is simultaneously a deconstruction and celebration of rock 'n' roll. The material draws on every version of the show so far, but is not, in many ways, the show that began a year ago. That blueprint was for a durational piece about noise bands and authenticity. This is a shorter, tighter and more linear piece.

Gemma is now the frontman, Rockstar Concentrate, and James plays a techie. Their conflict has moved into the centre of the piece: the techie refuses to watch the frontman/woman no matter how much she turns up the volume or works for the audience's love. Instead, he gazes at the floor as he manipulates the analogue synthesiser, which generates sounds that seem to pummel the earth itself.

Fierce Festival ➡

Three months later, I watch the production at the Fierce Festival in Birmingham.

The entrance is staffed by a fluorescent-jacketed security guard. The lady on the ticket desk gives me earplugs, and as I walk into the space itself, there is nothing to suggest that I haven't come to see a gig. The venue is packed to capacity. Two hundred people, mostly in their twenties, are standing on three sides of a small stage, drinking beer from plastic cups that they drop on the sticky floor, and talking over grunge and rock hits from the PA.

James is onstage already. He appears in the unassuming guise of the roadie. He repositions the microphone stand, tests the mic and checks the synth.

A one-two punch of Nirvana's 'In Bloom' and Guns N' Roses' 'Welcome to the Jungle' get heads bopping and helps to conjure the ritual of the gig. A group by the front of the stage starts to mosh.

The Frontman (Gemma) is all confidence and banter at the start. She lip-syncs to an Elvis song and flirts with the audience. The performance develops and she starts to lose control, as the techie, silent at first, shifts the sound from classic rock – shocking in its day, but now safe, even quaint – towards noise-core. She hands him the stage and when he accepts her challenge, she heckles from the bar and tries to turn the audience against him. They fight. The Frontman smashes her tambourine into the floor until nothing is left but splinters and flakes of lacquer. The sound and light builds to white noise.

A woman next to me walks out. A Home Counties-looking woman in her late fifties, wearing a trendy sari, she arrived early and inadvertently annoyed me with a loud, fifteen-minute monologue of dropped names from the theatre world, all in response to one of her friends asking simply, 'How are you?' Halfway in, she gives up. The performance has shut her down, and she has retreated into herself, unwilling to give any more. She looks around for some support, some other confused face. Seeing none, she rolls her eyes and walks out.

To get anything out of *Frontman*, an audience must meet it halfway. It must be willing to decipher and to make interpretative leaps. Months later, James will write a blog entitled 'Feedback for Audiences', in which he will explain that, like the founders of the DIY punk movement who inspired the piece, he is not interested in a financial transaction with the audience so much as the opportunity to collaborate with it. 'We promise to do the bulk of the work,' he will argue – 'after all, the audience pays to be entertained – but the audience has its "side of the bargain" to keep.' He will ask that audiences 'Listen, look and don't be frightened. Be here because you want to be here or don't come.'

A Cottage Industry ➡

A DIY ethic runs through Action Hero's work, not only in a homespun, lo-fi aesthetic, but in the means of production itself. Until recently, James and Gemma did everything as a pair, from booking venues to designing the publicity to performing. 'We have become a cottage industry,' Gemma says.

How Action Hero makes and tours work began as a necessity. 'We couldn't afford a tour-booker or a producer or a manager or an administrator,' Gemma says. 'If we wanted to have a flyer, we had to make one.' With *Frontman*, the company employed a producer for the first time, for 'temporary structural support', for five days' work to help with bookings. The company structure is now a choice, and a 'massively empowering' one to gain freedom and control over the work itself and how the work is communicated.

Savviness

Gemma and James know what Action Hero does, and what it doesn't do. 'We're won't create a show simply because someone thinks it's the "type" of show that might sustain a fifty-date tour,' James says.

The company is streamlined to make its work possible: it is two people, who have no interest in set texts, which means they have no performance rights to pay, and who live in Bristol, which is a large city but cheaper to live in than, say, London.

A small company has to tour to make even a meagre living. 'You have to take the work to people, which means getting out there to perform,' Gemma says.

> There is no sense in making a show that you'll never be able to present. As artists, you try not to let anything limit what you can make, but until recently, a show wasn't feasible for us if it couldn't be packed up in a small van, or if it needed to tour with a dedicated technician.

Gemma explains that, to get work made, a company has to make tough decisions:

> If you want theatre to be your career, you must be savvy because, whilst a big part of your career is making the best work you can, there's a whole other part, which is making decisions that are going to enable and support what you want to do, and finding a model that works for you.

The challenge, James explains, is to dissolve those parameters, and make work that can transport an audience to the Wild West, or to a daredevil stunt, or the doomed comeback gig given by the ghost of rock 'n' roll herself, and ask the audience to complete the story.

'If you resist an audience, you may as well be performing in your bedroom.'

Epilogue ➡
Asking Better Questions

I wrote at the start that this book would be about asking better questions. The process of creating theatre is often messy and difficult, and can seem and feel random.

Imagine that you are walking in a park in winter beside a frozen lake. Someone falls through the ice, and a bystander shouts for you to *act*. You would know what he meant.

Imagine that you are trying to explain to someone how you feel, or telling a friend how to drive to your house, and they ask you to be *direct*. You would know what they meant.

Imagine that you work in a restaurant, and the manager asks you to help *design* a menu or a process for organising the backroom staff. You would know what she meant.

Or imagine that your friend comes to you and confesses, beer in hand, that he took home a beautiful stranger from a club last night but failed to *perform*.

In so many contexts, these words – 'act', 'direct', 'design' and 'perform' – are clear, yet they are often contentious in theatre. For some, to attempt to agree a definition of the director's responsibilities, or even pose the question, represents a heretical failure of imagination. Indeed, the training and practice of a theatre director is more nebulous than most professions.

However, I believe that we might arrive at some principles to help the emerging director find focus, decide what projects to take, and create work that excites him.

Be yourself

Theatre directors describe themselves variously as problem-solvers, artists, editors, auteurs and collaborators. Some arrive at rehearsal with armfuls of secondary research, whilst others look only to the text. Some talk in concepts, others in minutiae. Some have a near-finished production in their heads from day one, others build and revise with their team. Some decline to socialise with their companies, and others drink with them into the early hours.

The directors in this book are different people, professionally and after-hours, and their lives and aesthetic interests are as much a part of their work as any list of exercises they might use in the rehearsal room. As we wrapped up interviews about *Troilus and Cressida*, Matthew Dunster reflected on his journey as an emerging director to find his voice. The only way to fail outright, he said, is to fake who you are:

> The only way to be 'found out' is if you're trying to fake your energy. No one can get away with it: it's exhausting and it divides your concentration when there's already enough in the rehearsal room to worry about. But more importantly, why would you want to fake your energy? Also, remember that a director only knows of a play what he knows of the world. You only know as much of, say, *Hamlet* or *King Lear* as you have experienced, and

what falls out of the text when you shake it depends on
that, which is why a director might direct *King Lear* in
his thirties then go back to it in his sixties.

The bad news is that you will never be a better Joe Hill-
Gibbins or Natalie Abrahami or whomever, than Joe
Hill-Gibbins or Natalie Abrahami, because you are not
them, and they are still making work. Imagine you went
up against Joe for a job and pitched your own Joe-like
production. Who would win?

The good news is that no one else is better at being *you*.
All art is specific to its creators, and one of the joys of
creating art is knowing that, were you to stop work on a
project, no one could complete it quite like you. It might
be good – it might be as good or even better than what
you would have done – but it wouldn't be the *same*.

Focus on what you want

Carrie Cracknell used an interesting turn of phrase
when I asked how her approach to directing has developed with experience. She said that, whilst her aesthetic
remains more or less constant, she is now more able to
help actors create 'the kind of work I'm interested in'.

That qualifier – 'the kind of work *I'm interested in*' –
suggests to me the tremendous agency behind the director's work. By contrast, I remember watching a
work-in-progress showing by an emerging director in
which the actors seemed to be performing in stylistically
different productions, and wandered aimlessly around
the stage. The director said afterwards that he didn't
want to 'impose himself' either on the text or the company. The performance was incoherent, boring, and the
director may as well have not turned up.

Steven Atkinson, the artistic director of HighTide Festival Theatre, says that part of what separates a play that

might make an impact from 'just another production' is the 'kind of arrogance' of a director who believes himself to be the only person who can tell that particular story 'as it needs to be told':

> If you read a play and you don't have a strong feeling about it, or if you think 'Oh, this could be done any number of ways' or 'I'd love to see Director X's version of this', then it is the wrong play for you. You should feel so strongly about a piece you want to direct that, if people don't like the production, you can say that you gave it the shot it deserved.

Focus also relates to a professional persona. Effective directors know the importance of defining their professional persona. Early in your career, it can be tempting to say 'yes' to every job that comes along, if only because it's flattering to be asked and you can't be certain when another will come. The result is anaemic rehearsed readings of plays directed by people who don't feel particularly excited by the script, and work that offers little insight. The immediate counter-argument might be that a director who is already successful is more able to turn down work. But usually, they turned down work even when they couldn't afford to, because they had some idea of the trajectory they wanted to create for themselves.

The fringe is full of directors producing their own plays, whose CVs cut across acting, directing, design and stage management. But a jumbled CV does not make a person appear as a tenacious polymath. Rather, a collision of genres and jobs too often betrays a lack of direction. No one wants to work with the guy who thinks he can 'write and sing the theme tune,' Steve Marmion said during our conversations about *Dick Whittington*. Steve, like most of the directors in this book, has other skills that he keeps off his directing CV. Many people have a hidden talent. It's not always a bad idea to keep it separate.

Be savvy

Two of the most unhelpful stereotypes of the 'true artist' are that he must be wiry and awkward, and that he must consider business the antithesis of art.

In conversation with the directors, two words kept coming back: 'savvy' and 'adaptive'. To work as a professional theatremaker is not only to have good ideas and deliver effective notes, but to survive in a saturated industry.

More often than not, you will be responsible for delivering a production that has been paid for with someone else's money, says Steven Atkinson, who happily uses words like 'critical capital' and 'collateral' to describe good press:

> A large part of directing is risk management. The most fragile point in any show is when it's in rehearsal and, if a producer is giving you money, they want to know that you can be trusted with their investment. Producers want to know: 'Can this person manage the room? Can they deliver the project on budget and on time? Can they collaborate?' When you present yourself as a director, not only must you have a vision for what you're going to achieve, but a plan for how you're going to do it. You must instil the belief that you can do what you say you're going to do.

Savviness means knowing the industry, which includes knowing how roles operate within it and how theatres are funded. Steven attributes part of HighTide's success to the fact that, whilst his fellow students at university focused solely on writers and directors, he would flip one page back in the printed script and take note of the theatre staff. 'You should know not only the stars of theatre, but its backbone,' he says. You may know that Peter Brook directed a seminal production of *A Midsummer Night's Dream* at the Royal Shakespeare Company in 1970, but Steven could tell you who employed Brook and who was running the marketing department. Years later, he would draw on that kind of knowledge to assemble the board of HighTide. Instead of firing letters to the artistic director of the National Theatre or the chief executive of the Arts Council, he focused on reaching people he might have a chance of reaching, and asked them to advocate for him.

Take responsibility

Simply consider these four comments:

- 'Invariably, if the problem with a scene is the acting, the cause is the direction. At the end of the day, if there's something in the production that I'm not happy with, it's my fault and no one else's.' *Natalie Abrahami*
- 'I take responsibility for everything that happens in my rehearsal room, good or bad.' *Matthew Dunster*
- 'It took me ten years to accept that, if you look at the show and it's not what you wanted it to be, it's no one's fault but your own.' *Steve Marmion*
- 'When I commission a writer, I set the boundaries of the attempt, so the text that ends up onstage is my responsibility as well. Once you take that on-board, it stops you punishing other people or circumstances when things don't happen as you wanted. Let that responsibility empower you.' *Carrie Cracknell*

Theatre is resource-intensive

Sometimes I am jealous of my friend Felix, who works as a photographer. When Felix goes to work, he often straps a camera over his shoulder and heads out on to the street. If he's photographing an event, there is little to set up because the event is happening anyway. When he has taken his photos, he can put them online and an editor can decide quickly whether to hire him.

Compare theatre: the director needs space and actors, both of which are expensive, and if he wants someone – a critic, a mentor, a potential employer – to come, he needs to convince them to leave their house and give an evening of their time.

Theatremaking is people- and resource-intensive. A director who resents this fact is in the wrong profession. Theatre is a conversation between many voices, and a director who doesn't like people, or who swears he does his best work away from the group, is as fundamentally broken as a pilot who hates to fly.

Don't be a jerk

As director, your mood permeates the rehearsal room and the production itself. It indicates the strength of feeling on this issue that more than half of the directors I spoke to used words to describe tyrannical or conde-scending directors that many of them would otherwise avoid. 'A shit director can spoil everything,' Steve Marmion added. 'No one gets paid enough in this indus-try to have a horrible time.'

The jerk director thinks he is necessarily the smartest person in the room. He treats actors as marionettes and he bellows or is passive-aggressive, thinking that his cre-ativity excuses his lack of civility. He thinks the industry owes him, or, tired by the world's indifference, he becomes bitter and decides that his work – even his soul – is too avant-garde, too 'daring' to succeed in a world that has deadened itself with trashy, reality TV.

Don't be a jerk.

Collaborate with the creative team and the company

The opposite of being a jerk is being a collaborator. How you set the boundaries of the collaboration will depend on who you are, but what should remain constant is the belief that an expert in their field – design, sound, light, costume, dramaturgy – can take whatever you have conceived and notch it up a level.

Steven Atkinson of HighTide again:

> I have a clear vision of any play I direct: what the audience's role will be within the work, and how I want the audience to engage with it. This feeds the parameters of the show and certain staging choices (end-on, site specific, etc.). Within that, I try to be collaborative and encourage the actors to take ownership of their performances. If you can't let go of that, you should do something else. That's not even an artistic decision, that's a life decision: it is masochistic to do something that pains you.

There are emerging directors who view creative teams as an unfortunate reflection of the fact that they haven't the time to do it all themselves. These people are jerks.

When you engage a creative team, find the smartest people you can find, and listen to their counsel.

There is another reason to collaborate, which has to do with your career development. To direct professionally is to engage with the machinery of the theatre industry. The director who also wants to design and produce every show not only endangers the quality of the work, but shows to the world that she cannot get along with other people. It will be difficult for an employer to suspect anything other than that she likes to lead a team of one because she knows she will win every argument. If you behave that way, think of the people you won't meet, and who won't be able to help develop your practice, and vice versa.

Accept no defaults

At its most fundamental, the director's job is to tell the story. Everything else is up for grabs.

There is a strong literary tradition in British theatre. There are even those who argue that to present a piece of theatre that is anything other than a traditional play staged behind a proscenium arch represents a deviation that requires its own justification.

The chapter on *The Glass Menagerie* made the case that a singular production cannot be derived from a text. I would add that an interesting production invariably starts with as few defaults as possible. Where there is a text, the process begins by interrogating its words and asking what might be the most effective way of delivering this story?

Every few months, a journalist writes an article or a blog that questions whether something they've just seen 'is or isn't theatre'. Is it theatre to bake bread onstage? Is it theatre to watch a motorcyclist attempt a circus-style Wall of Death? But the question is boring and I wonder if the propensity to ask it often marks a divide between artists and people who write about art. When I asked James Stenhouse from Action Hero how I should refer to *Frontman*, he shrugged. 'Live art? Performance? Theatre? Whatever.'

We would do well to remember Matthew Dunster's definition of theatricality: 'One group of people presenting something to another group of people who are watching.' (Of course, the audience need not only watch.) Beyond that, who cares how someone chooses to define it?

Keep up to date with the industry

There is no golden age of creativity that has passed. The history of theatre does not end with the last 'great text' studied in universities or written about in newspapers. Interesting people are making exciting things all the time and the director has a duty to remain fascinated and buoyed by the ongoing stream of human creativity.

Intelligent isn't enough

The ability to write an essay on a play's meaning and know where it sits in the canon does not mean that a director can necessarily conceive an interesting production, by which I mean a production that feeds the senses and expands words into three-dimensional space. Nor does abstract intelligence suggest that a director has the bedside manner to engender trust and develop strategies to enable the creativity of others. It is true that many successful directors possess a scholarly intelligence, but this is not all they possess. Invariably there is instinct and emotional intelligence.

Make work for audiences

Most audiences are interested in stories, and could not care less for process any more than I am interested in the inner workings of the word-processing software I'm using right now. I'm sure we will agree that the most powerful art – whatever we each take 'powerful' to mean – escapes simple categorisation, but the further one moves towards the professional director, the less one hears words like 'intangible', 'idiosyncratic', 'difficult', 'ineffable' or even 'artistic', and more one hears words like 'clear', 'specific', 'useful', 'helpful', 'compelling', 'engaging' and 'satisfying'.

The latter set of words has two benefits over the former. First, it puts the audience's experience ahead of the artist's desire for self-expression. Second, it sets more quantifiable goals. Whether a scene feels 'artistic' is difficult to answer. Whether it is 'engaging' and 'compelling' is less so, and is more useful in driving rehearsal.

To make the audience the arbitrator of your work helps also to 'mitigate directorly, actorly and writerly egos,' Steve Marmion says. 'You can bring everything back to one question: "What effect do we want to have on the audience?"'

'A director needs to learn what the audience needs,' Natalie Abrahami said after a preview performance of *A Midsummer Night's Dream*, as she considered the pace and rhythm of the production so far. 'If you pay attention, the audience will tell you where you need to open the play out or take off the stabilisers.'

Nailing the production in rehearsal

You may have heard the old nonsense: 'Lousy dress run, great first night.' That should be: 'Lousy dress run, lousy first night.' To add a corollary: 'If a scene is not funny/thrilling/suspenseful to the five people lining the walls of the rehearsal room, the presence of a full house is unlikely to correct it magically.'

As Joe Hill-Gibbins explained during tech for *The Glass Menagerie*, a rehearsal process is unusually fluid, with no element of the production locked down as it would be in, say, film. However, a production progresses in stages, each adding a layer. Unless the production is strong at the end of each stage, it will start to slip out from under the director and the company:

279

- Having chosen a text, or a stimulus to devise, you should have no doubt that you have chosen something compelling.

- Having assembled the creative team and cast, you should have no doubt that you have chosen a team that challenges you, and who will enrich and develop your concept.

- At the end of the early stages of rehearsal, there should be a shared understanding of what the production intends to achieve.

- At the end of the tech process, the production should be physically safe for the actors to perform.

- To adapt the old military phrase: no plan survives engagement with the audience. By the end of the preview process, you should have made whatever alterations to the production you feel are necessary so that it is the strongest possible version of itself.

- After press night, you should be able to leave the production confident that it reflects everyone's best work.

Forget about money

Perhaps fifty per cent of conversations between emerging directors turn quickly to frustration about money. Most are reasoned concerns about the costs inherent in housing companies in suitable buildings for long enough to generate meaningful work, and more than a few are tirades about how empty buildings owned by 'wanker bankers' should be turned over to artists such as themselves (usually employing the tautologous logic that art matters because it matters).

The reality is that few people who make theatre sustain a living from doing so. To be happy in this industry, you must sever any connection between money and self-worth. In some industries, people compete for high salaries and pension plans and company cars. Emerging directors often compete for unpaid work.

Before you devote yourself to this path, ask yourself: 'How will I live? How much work do I need to be doing to be happy?'

One day during tech at the Lyric Hammersmith, Steve Marmion's mum dropped by. She told me that she suspected her son might have quit theatre altogether had he not been offered the job of artistic director of Soho Theatre. I put that to Steve a few months later. He said it was true and that I could quote her:

> I'm not annoyed at the industry for not giving me 'a break' because no one's owed that, but I was having a fair stab at it. I was getting tired of having one idea in twenty work out, and directing drama-school and youth-theatre productions that I wasn't learning from. I've had some nice things in the diary, but is a panto and one fringe show a year enough to make you stay? Theatre is a tough way to make a living. There aren't enough jobs for the people in it already, and there's no money in it, so unless you *need* to go into theatre, don't, because you will wonder why you didn't choose to lose your mind for something else. Directing is a weird, lone-wolf existence. I have many reasons why I think it's *important*, but I don't know why *I* have to do it. When you do switch off? I'm yet to work that one out.

Riding shotgun with the theatremakers in this book has rubbed away almost all the gold that theatre once had for me. But either you fall in love with the nickel underneath, or you do something else. This is the difference between infatuation and love.

The director's graft

Matthew Dunster told me when we first met that a goal of directing his first Shakespeare production, *Macbeth*, which came directly before *Troilus and Cressida*, was to survive the experience. The lessons he learned on that production he developed in *Troilus and Cressida* and his experiences on *Troilus and Cressida* fed into a production of *The Two Gentlemen of Verona*, which he directed at the Royal and Derngate, Northampton, and so on.

Matthew praised the 'wisdom' of emerging directors who develop their work 'at a steady pace', and who are not focused on fast-track graduate programmes or being hailed as the next wunderkind of British theatre:

> One of the reasons I always bang on about football is
> that managers don't manage clubs straight out of
> university. Most have been players and they're reaching
> the end of their footballing career. They have eight or
> ten years of life under their belt; of having someone
> kicking their head in. You have to know your onions.

Steve Marmion, who started his career teaching, also stressed the importance of allowing one's self to develop, and trusting that you will:

> When I assisted directors like Rupert Goold and
> Gordon Anderson earlier in my career, I would watch
> them find details and make observations that I was sure
> I would never find – but the more you work, the more
> keys you add to your chain and the more nimbly you
> find them. You must trust that you will get wiser.

How then to make one's first steps in the industry, or situate one's work between, at one end of the spectrum, the mundane, and at the other, the impenetrable confusion of forms, colours and noises?

I confess that, when I started, I was looking for a few answers; for some hard science behind the alchemy.

Even a few quick fixes and silver bullets. But there are none. Returning to my email archive to fish out some past correspondence between Matthew Dunster and me, I stumble across the second email he sent me, days after we met:

> There is no process really. Just keep talking to people, keep asking questions and keep pushing everyone – especially yourself.

I'm sorry if you were expecting an answer. I cannot give you that, although neither can the masters, who can tell you only how they came to find what works for them. Anything that is of merit will come from you and will be, at least in one small way, unlike what has come before.

However, we can ask smarter questions, which is what I hope this book has been about. We can ask smarter questions of ourselves, of each other and of scripts, and of the form itself.

Now go make something.

Other Books for Directors ➡

THE ACTING BOOK
John Abbott

THE IMPROVISATION BOOK
How to Conduct Successful Improvisation Sessions
John Abbott

IMPROVISATION IN REHEARSAL
John Abbott

DIFFERENT EVERY NIGHT
Freeing the Actor
Mike Alfreds

INVENTING THE TRUTH
Devising and Directing for the Theatre
Mike Bradwell

THE RELUCTANT ESCAPOLOGIST
Adventures in Alternative Theatre
Mike Bradwell

 **from Nick Hern Books**

THE ACTOR AND THE TARGET
Declan Donnellan

WORDS INTO ACTION
Finding the Life of the Play
William Gaskill

HOUSE OF GAMES
Making Theatre from Everyday Life
Chris Johnston

THE IMPROVISATION GAME
Discovering the Secrets of Spontaneous Performance
Chris Johnston

TAKING STOCK
Philip Roberts *and* Max Stafford-Clark

LETTERS TO GEORGE
Max Stafford-Clark